THE BIGGEST,
FUNNIEST, WACKIEST, GROSSEST
JOKE
BOOK
EVER!

THE BIGGEST, FUNNIEST, WACKIEST, GROSSEST

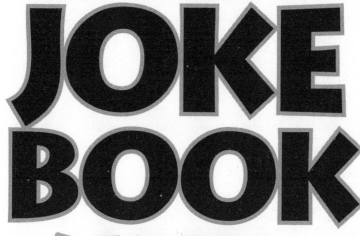

JOKE BOOK EVER!

Editors of Portable Press

PORTABLE
PRESS

San Diego, California

Portable Press
An imprint of Printers Row Publishing Group
10350 Barnes Canyon Road, Suite 100, San Diego, CA 92121
www.portablepress.com • mail@portablepress.com

Printer Row Publishing Group is a division of Readerlink Distribution Services.
Portable Press is a registered trademark of Readerlink Distribution Services, LLC.

The Biggest, Funniest, Wackiest, Grossest Joke Book Ever!
is a compilation of the following previously published titles:
The Funniest Joke Book Ever!, © 2016
Cover and interior concept by Patrick Merrell
The Grossest Joke Book Ever!, © 2016
Cover and interior concept by Patrick Merrell
The Wackiest Joke Book Ever!, © 2017
Cover and interior concept by Patrick Merrell
Collected and curated by Kim Griswell
The Funniest Knock-Knock Jokes Ever!, © 2017
Cover and interior concept by Patrick Merrell
Collected and curated by Kim Griswell

Correspondence regarding the content of this book should be sent to
Portable Press, Editorial Department, at the above address.

Publisher: Peter Norton • Associate Publisher: Ana Parker
Publishing/Editorial Team: Vicki Jaeger, Tanja Fijalkowski,
Stephanie Romero Gamboa, Kathryn C. Dalby, Lauren Taniguchi
Editorial Team: JoAnn Padgett, Melinda Allman, J. Carroll, Dan Mansfield
Production Team: Jonathan Lopes, Rusty von Dyl

Interior: SunDried Penguin

Library of Congress Cataloging-in-Publication Data

Names: Portable Press (San Diego, Calif.), editor.
Title: The biggest, funniest, wackiest, grossest joke book ever! / editors of Portable Press.
Description: San Diego, California : Portable Press, [2020] I Summary: "A four-in-one book
    collection that features hundreds of Q&As, puns, wisecracks, knock-knock jokes, and much
    more for kids of all ages."-- Provided by publisher.
Identifiers: LCCN 2019059732 I ISBN 9781645173755 (hardcover) I ISBN 9781645175032 (ebook)
Subjects: LCSH: Wit and humor, Juvenile.
Classification: LCC PN6166.B54 2020 I DDC 818/.60208--dc23
LC record available at https://lccn.loc.gov/2019059732

Printed in the United States of America

24 23 22 21 20 1 2 3 4 5

CONTENTS

FAMILY FUNNIES

Why was the mother firefly unhappy?

Her children weren't very bright.

What does the Pickle family do when their car breaks down?

They dill with it.

Why did the kid leave cheese beside the computer?

To feed the mouse.

Mom: Did you take a shower this morning?

Kid: Why? Is one missing?

Sis: When did you lose your two front teeth?

Bro: I didn't. They're in my pocket.

Who is bigger, Mrs. Bigger or her baby?

Her baby is a little Bigger.

Dad: Why did you fail your history test?

Kid: All the questions were about things that happened before I was born.

Mama Giraffe: Eat your leaves, son. They put color in your cheeks.

Giraffe Son: Who wants green cheeks?

Why wasn't Mom worried about the moose in the kitchen?

It was a chocolate mousse.

Elephant Baby: Pops, do elephants really have good memories?

Elephant Dad: I forget.

If you eat one half of an apple pie and your sister eats the other half, what are you left with?

A very angry mom.

Why did Ed's parents name their second son Ed, too?

Because two Eds are better than one.

Bro: I just spotted a leopard!

Sis: Don't be silly. Leopards are born that way.

Why don't dads ever buy new underwear?

Because *under*wear never gets worn *out*.

Grandma: I once typed an essay on the belly of a frog.

Grandkid: Wow! How'd you get the frog into the typewriter?

What's the best cure for sleepwalking?

Put tacks on the floor.

Dad: Why did you dip your computer in melted caramel?

Kid: I wanted a candied Apple.

How can you tell a baby snake?

By its rattle.

Why did Grandpa's hair turn gray before his moustache?

It was older.

Mom: I found a restaurant where we can eat dirt cheap!

Dad: I'd rather eat steak.

Who isn't your sister or brother but is still a child of your parents?

You.

What did the mama cow say to her calf?

"Go to sleep! It's pasture bedtime."

Hey! There's a family of horses moving in next door!

Great! They'll make good nei-ei-ei-ghbors.

How many paws does a lion have?

One Paw. Just like everyone else.

What happened when the baby drank 8 colas?

He burped 7-Up.

Dad: Why are you eating your homework?

Kid: The teacher said it was a piece of cake.

What happened when Mom put too much mousse in her hair?

She grew antlers.

Why was the kid late to school every day?

The teacher said it was never too late to learn.

What's worse than a crying baby?

Two crying babies.

What did the mirror say to the dresser?

"I see your drawers!"

Why did Farmer John borrow a needle from his wife?

He couldn't find the one in the haystack.

Why did the kid put the cake in the freezer?

It needed icing.

Kid: How many apples grow on a tree?

Mom: All of them.

Do you have to be royal to ride in a carriage?

Not if you're a baby.

Which family member is purple?

Your grape-grandmother.

Kid: Dad, which board do you need to finish the fence?

Dad: The last one.

Which relatives always come to family picnics?

The ants.

Which grade should you never get on a report card?

D. It makes Ma mad.

What is big and yellow and comes in the morning
to brighten Mom's day?

The school bus.

Why did Dad work late at the pajama factory?

He was on the nightie shift.

Kid: What's the best way to avoid wrinkles?

Grandma: Don't sleep in your clothes.

Kid: Will the pancakes be long? I'm starving.

Dad: No. They'll be round.

What do you call rotten eggs, spoiled milk,
and moldy bread?

Gross-eries.

Mom: How do you know the dog ate your homework?

Kid: I fed it to him.

What do you give a sick female relative?

Auntie-biotics.

**Grandpa: I've been swimming since
I was five years old.**

Grandkid: You must be really tired.

Put your grandma on speed dial.

Boom: Insta-Gram!

Kid: Will you remember me tomorrow?

Mom: Of course.

Kid: Will you remember me next week?

Mom: Yes.

Kid: Will you remember me next month?

Mom: Absolutely.

Kid: Will you remember me next year?

Mom: Without a doubt.

Kid: Knock-knock!

Mom: Who's there?

Kid: You forgot me already?

Brother: Is there a hole in your shoe?

Sister: No.

Brother: Then how did you get your foot into it?

What do whales chew?

Blubber gum.

What is black and white and green and black and white?

Two zebras fighting over a pickle.

What kind of animal lives in a can?

A cantaloupe.

Why did the elephant quit the circus?

He was tired of working for peanuts.

Who wrote *The Worst Joke Book Ever*?

Terry Bull.

What is white on the top, yellow in the middle, and white on the bottom?

A lion sandwich.

What is black and white and red all over?

A zebra hiding in a bottle of ketchup.

How are playing cards like wolves?

They both travel in packs.

What one-horned animal won't take "no" for an answer?

The why-nocerous.

Why do giraffes have such long necks?

Because their feet stink.

Why did the watchdog sleep all the time?

His owner forgot to wind him.

Why are there no aardvarks in Alaska?

They can't afford the plane fare.

What was the silly chicken doing in the garden?

Sitting on an eggplant.

What do you call a dog that sneezes?

A germy shepherd.

THE WACKIEST JOKES EVER!

What do you call a bunny that gives out parking tickets?

Meter Rabbit.

Why wouldn't the horse talk to the cow?

Everything she said was udder nonsense.

Where do cows go on vacation?

Moo York.

Why did the hippo sit on a pumpkin?

He wanted to play squash.

What do baby bunnies learn in school?

The alfalfa-bet.

What's the difference between a platypus and a peanut butter sandwich?

A platypus doesn't stick to the roof of your mouth.

Why do squirrels live in trees?

To avoid all the nuts on the ground.

How do dogs keep up on local news?

Smellovision.

ANIMAL SILLIES

How does a polite lion greet a hunter?
"Pleased to eat you!"

What is the biggest ant?
The elephant!

Which animal never remembers names?
The owl. It's always saying, "Who? Who?"

What's the best use of cowhide?
To keep the cow together.

How do you know there's an elephant in your sandwich?
It's too heavy to lift.

How do fish buy things online?
With a credit cod.

Which bird is always out of breath?
A puffin.

Why did the dog go to jail?
He didn't pay his barking ticket.

Why do rabbits have fur coats?
Because they'd look silly in leather jackets.

THE WACKIEST JOKES EVER!

Why don't polar bears live in the desert?

They can't bear the heat.

How many kinds of gnus are there?

Two. Good gnus and bad gnus.

What do you call an elephant in a phone booth?

Stuck.

How can you keep milk from spoiling?

Leave it in the cow.

How can you tell which end of a worm is its head?

Tickle it in the middle and see which end laughs.

What do you get if you cross a barber with a sheep?

A baa-aa-aad haircut.

How do you get fur from a bear?

Run as fast as you can!

Why did the ram fall off the cliff?

It didn't see the ewe turn.

What is a skunk's favorite sandwich?
Peanut butter and smelly.

Why did the cow stop giving milk?
She wasn't in the moooooo-d.

What do you call a canine magician?
A labracadabrador.

Why do ducks make the best detectives?
They always quack the case.

What did the nearsighted porcupine say to the cactus?
"Hi, Mom!"

What do alligators call children?
Appetizers.

What do dogs eat at the movies?
Pupcorn.

SILLYSAURUS

What kind of dinosaur wears a cowboy hat and boots?

Tyrannosaurus tex.

Why did the raptor paint its claws yellow?

So it could hide in the banana tree.

What goes *thump, squish, thump, squish*?

A T. rex with one wet sneaker.

Which dinosaur has the biggest vocabulary?

A Thesaurus.

What is a dinosaur's favorite snack?

Macaroni and trees.

Which dinosaur demolishes buildings?

Tyrannosaurus wrecks.

What do you call a dinosaur that stubs its toe?

Sore-toe-a-saurus.

Did you hear the one about the pterodactyl egg?

It was a very old yolk.

Why did the plesiosaur eat a fleet of ships carrying potatoes?

Because no one can eat just one potato ship.

What do you get when you cross a dinosaur and a wizard?

Tyrannosaurus hex.

What was the world's fastest dinosaur?

The prontosaurus.

How do you tell a dinosaur to hurry?

"Shake a leg-osaurus!"

Why are dinosaurs big, green, and scaly?

If they were small, yellow, and fuzzy, they would be tennis balls.

Why did the stegosaurus climb a tree?

Because the sign said KEEP OFF THE GRASS.

What is T. rex's favorite game?

Swallow the leader.

Why did the pterodactyl cross the road?
Because there weren't any chickens yet.

Why shouldn't you teach T. rex to add 4 + 4?
You might get 8 (ate).

Which dinosaur keeps you awake at night?
The bronto-snore-us.

What follows a stegosaurus wherever it goes?
Its tail.

What do you get if you give a dinosaur a pogo stick?
Big holes in your driveway.

What do you call the king of the dinosaurs after it evolves into a chicken?
Tyrannosaurus pecks.

Why did the sauropod wear purple pajamas?
Because its pink ones were in the wash.

What kind of dinosaur has no wings, but flies all over?
The kind that needs a bath.

How do you get down from a dinosaur?

You don't! You get down from a goose.

What time is it when a dinosaur sits on your toilet?

Time to get a new toilet.

Which dinosaur was a crybaby?

Tear-annosaurus rex.

What do you do with a yellow triceratops?

Teach it to be brave.

What was the brontosaurus's favorite game?

Squash.

What does a triceratops sit on?

Its tricera-bottom.

Why did T. rex cross the road?

To eat the chickens on the other side.

What do you call a polite dinosaur?

A please-iosaur.

Why are dinosaurs always found in the ground?

Because they couldn't climb trees.

Which dinosaur caught the worm?
Archaeopteryx. It was an early bird.

What kind of dinosaurs live in graveyards?
Cemetery-dactyls.

Why do museums have so many old dinosaur bones?
They can't find any new ones.

Why did the dinosaur eat a cow and three ducks?
It liked milk and quackers.

What do you do when a dinosaur breaks its toe?
Call a very big toe truck.

What do you call a T. rex having a temper tantrum?
Brat-T. rex.

Why invite a dinosaur to your birthday party?
They're tons of fun.

Why did dinosaurs become extinct?
They didn't want to hear any more dinosaur jokes.

Where was the dinosaur when the sun went down?
In the dark.

Why did the apatosaurus devour the factory?

She was a plant eater.

Which dinosaurs make the best police officers?

Tricera-cops.

When is a dinosaur likely to enter your house?

When the door is open.

What's bright blue and weighs 2,000 pounds?

A dinosaur holding its breath.

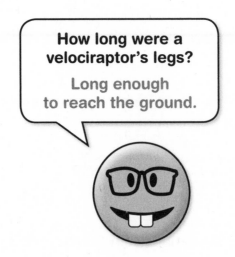

How long were a velociraptor's legs?

Long enough to reach the ground.

How do you make a hot dog stand?
Steal its chair.

What is the first thing a ball does when it stops rolling?
It looks round.

What do you call a six-foot-tall basketball player?
Shortie.

What is stranger than seeing a catfish?
Seeing a goldfish bowl.

What can you serve but never eat?
A tennis ball.

Why are baseball games played at night?
Because bats sleep during the day.

What's the bounciest room in a palace?
The ballroom.

Why did the umpire throw the chicken out of the game?

He suspected fowl play.

Why can't pigs play basketball?

They hog the ball.

What are the last words of "The Star Spangled Banner"?

Play ball!

Why are fish lousy at volleyball?

They run away from the net.

What is harder to catch the faster you run?

Your breath.

What does an umpire always do before he eats?

Brushes off the plate.

Soccer player: I could kick myself for missing that goal.

Teammate: Don't bother. You'll probably miss.

What did the batter say when the coach called in a new pitcher?

"That's a relief!"

How is a baseball catcher like a farmer?
They both chase fowls.

Why are basketballs always wet?
The players dribble a lot.

Why do golfers like to eat Cheerios?
Because there's a hole in every one.

How are football players like pilots?
They both make touchdowns.

What's the difference between a bad goalie and Cinderella?
Cinderella got to the ball.

Mom: Which player is the fullback?
Kid: The one who ate too much before the game.

Which three letters will stop a quarterback sneak?
I-C-U!

What bird can be found at the end of every race?
The puffin.

What did the dog say when a ball landed on top of the house?

"Roof! Roof!"

How do you keep squirrels off the football field?

Hide the ball. It drives them nuts!

Which sport is the quietest?

Bowling. You can hear a pin drop.

Wide receiver: What's the best way to catch a ball?

Coach: Have someone throw it to you.

Why did Cinderella lose the tennis tournament?

She had a pumpkin for a coach.

When do baseball players wear armor?

For knight games.

Golfer: Golf is a funny game.

Caddy: It's not supposed to be.

What is a basketball player's favorite kind of story?

Tall tales.

What's the funniest baseball team?

The New York Prankees.

What do you call a girl who stands in the middle of a volleyball court?

Annette.

Coach: You'd be better at bowling than baseball.

Kid: Why?

Coach: You always get strikes!

Why did the football fan go to the bathroom?

He wanted to watch the Toilet Bowl.

What's a basketball player's favorite snack?

Cookies, because they can dunk them.

Why did the baseball player keep winking?

He needed batting practice.

Why did the chicken cross the baseball field?

The umpire called a fowl.

Sports stories: *Extra Innings* by Willy Win, illustrated by Betty Wont

What has 18 legs and catches flies?

A baseball team.

Where do old bowling balls end up?

In the gutter.

How do hens root for their favorite football team?

They egg them on.

Why did the shortstop get arrested?

He was caught stealing third base.

Why do porcupines win every ball game?

They have the most points.

THAT'S HISTORICAL!

Who was America's funniest Founding Father?

Benjamin Pranklin.

Where was Queen Elizabeth II crowned?

On her head.

Teacher: For tonight's homework, write an essay on Abraham Lincoln.

Student: I'd rather write on paper.

Who was France's sleepiest emperor?

Nap-oleon.

Which American president wore the biggest shoes?

The one with the biggest feet.

Which Egyptian queen loved spaghetti?

Cleo-pasta.

How was Thomas Jefferson like a fish?

He was a flounder of his country.

THAT'S HISTORICAL!

Why did Paul Revere always carry a handkerchief?

He was the town crier.

Why was Queen Elizabeth I buried at Westminster Abbey?

Because she was dead.

Which patriotic song comes in handy when you sneeze?

Hanky Doodle Dandy.

What did Pocahontas become on her 21st birthday?

A year older.

Who invented the first airplane that didn't fly?

The Wrong brothers.

Who was purple and conquered the world?

Alexander the Grape.

Where is Timbuktu?

Between Timbuk-one and Timbuk-three.

Why did Teddy Roosevelt throw away his sleeping bag?

He couldn't get it to wake up.

Which president was the best social-networker?

Abraham LinkedIn.

How were the Pilgrims like ants?

They lived in colonies.

Which famous French landmark can't stand up?

The Eiffel (I fell) Tower.

What's the smelliest statue in Egypt?

The Stynx.

Which Leonardo da Vinci painting won't stop complaining?

The Moaning Lisa.

What did Benjamin Franklin say when he discovered electricity?

Nothing. He was too shocked.

Why didn't the lookout on the *Titanic* spot the iceberg?

He had bad ice-sight.

Which telephone inventor had a cookie named after him?

Alexander Graham Cracker.

Which Roman emperor always had a cold?

Julius Sneezer.

Who was the world's smartest pig?

Ein-swine.

What part of London is in China?

The letter "n."

If Genghis Khan were alive today, what would he be most famous for?

His age.

How did George Washington cross the Delaware?

In a boat.

Where can you find Moscow?

In the barn, next to Pa's cow.

What do Alexander the Great and Winnie the Pooh have in common?

Their middle name.

How often do ships like the *Titanic* sink?

Just once.

Two wrongs don't make a right, so what do two rights make?

An airplane.

What did Sir Lancelot wear to bed?

A knight gown.

Which soldiers traveled the most?

The Romans.

How is the United States like a healthy kid?

Both have good constitutions.

Why was Billy the Kid sitting on his mother's stove?

He wanted to be home on the range.

Where was the Treaty of 1783 signed?

At the bottom.

What happened when an apple hit Sir Isaac Newton on the head?

He realized the gravity of the situation.

Why don't you ever hear about Betsy Ross?

Interest in her has flagged.

Is the capital of Missouri pronounced Saint Loo-is or Saint Loo-ey?

Neither. It's pronounced Jefferson City.

How do we know the ancient Romans were smart?

They understood Latin.

What's the capital of Pennsylvania?

P.

How would a robber get gold out of Fort Knox?

Through the door.

What was the closest thing to King George III?

His underwear.

What happened to the inventor of sandpaper?

He had a rough time.

What stands in New York harbor and sneezes all day?

The Achoo of Liberty.

TOAD-ALLY WACKY

What is green and red all over?
A frog holding its breath.

Why couldn't the lizard stop singing?
He was a rap-tile.

What's green and bumpy and jumps a lot?
A cucumber with hiccups.

How do you catch a baby frog?
With a toad-pole.

How is a toad like a brick?
Neither one can play the trumpet.

What kind of lizard tells jokes?
A stand-up chameleon.

Why did the frog think it was a bird?
Because it was pigeon-toad.

What do you get when you cross a turtle with a sheep?

A turtle-neck sweater.

How many witches does it take to change a lightbulb?

One...but she changes it into a toad!

Diner: Waiter! Why is there a frog in my soup?

Waiter: Looks like it's eating the fly.

What do frogs always catch during baseball games?

Pop flies.

What do you get when you cross a toad with a pig?

A wart-hog.

What did the toad say to the kangaroo?

"I feel kinda jumpy today. How about you?"

What happens when you throw a toad into the ocean?

It gets toad-ally wet.

What do turtles do on their birthday?

Shellabrate!

What do you say if you meet a toad?

"Wart's new?"

What kind of frog can be found at the North Pole?

One that's toad-ally lost.

Why did the toad sit on a marshmallow?

So it wouldn't fall into the hot chocolate.

What's the funniest place in the frog pond?

The silly pad.

What do you get when you cross a toad with Luke Skywalker?

Star Warts.

Why can't you believe anything toads tell you?

They're am-*fib*-ians.

How do you get a frog to fly?

Buy it an airplane ticket.

What kind of slippers did Frogerella wear to the ball?

Open-toad.

What goes *ribbit, ribbit, thunk*?

A frog laughing its head off.

Why did the frog jump over the moon?

Because the cow was on vacation.

What did the frog say when it couldn't stop coughing?

"Sorry, I have a person in my throat."

What's green and warty and goes up and down all day?

A toad in an elevator.

What happens if you swallow a toad?

You croak!

Why did the frog take the bus?

Its car got toad.

Where do toads hang their coats?

In the croakroom.

What do you get if you cross a toad with a crocodile?

Leaping lizards.

What goes *dit-dit-dot-croak, dit-dit-dot-croak*?

Morse toad.

What's the best way to catch a tadpole?

Have someone throw it at you.

Why did the boy put a mouse in his sister's bed?

He couldn't catch a toad.

What do you get when you cross an alligator with a pickle?

A croco-dill.

What do toads drink in winter?

Hot croako.

THAT'S BANANAS!

Why did the elephant stomp on the banana?
He wanted a banana splat!

Why aren't bananas lonely?
They always travel in bunches.

What is King Kong's favorite musical?
Little Orphan Banannie.

How do monkeys get downstairs?
They slide down the banana-ster.

Why didn't the monkey undress for its bath?
Because it was wearing a bathrobe.

What's a monkey's favorite ice cream?
Chocolate chimp.

Which side of a monkey has the most fur?
The outside.

What is long and yellow and always points north?

A magnetic banana.

Which monkeys can fly?

Hot-air baboons.

Why couldn't the monkey open the piano?

The keys were inside.

What is yellow and wears a mask?

The Lone Banana.

What did the monkey say to the sleeping banana?

"Stop snoring before you wake up the whole bunch."

Moviegoer: I can't believe how much your monkey liked that movie.

Lady with monkey: I can't either!
He hated the book.

Why don't chimpanzees have tails?

So they won't get caught in revolving doors.

What's yellow and writes?

A ballpoint banana.

What do you call a monkey whose bananas were stolen?

Furious George.

What is yellow and goes up and down?

A banana in an elevator.

What kind of monkeys live at the North Pole?

Cold ones.

Why do monkeys have fur?

So their underwear won't show.

What did the banana say to the monkey?

Don't be silly—bananas can't talk!

What do you call two monkeys who hang over a window?

Kurt-n-Rod.

How do you keep a monkey from going through the eye of a needle?

Tie a knot in its tail.

Why did the monkey put banana peels on his feet?

He needed a new pair of slippers.

**What do you call a monkey that swims
with crocodiles?**

Dinner.

What's yellow and hairy?

A banana wearing a toupee.

**What should you do if you find ten little monkeys
sleeping on your bed?**

Get a hotel room.

Why did the monkey try to eat its bicycle?

It had a banana seat.

Where do you find monkeys?

Depends on where you left them.

What do you call a 2,000-pound gorilla?

Sir.

**Why did the monkey close its eyes when it
looked in the mirror?**

To see how it looked when it was asleep.

**What lives in a vineyard and swings through
the vines?**

Tarzan of the Grapes.

How long should a monkey's legs be?

Long enough to reach the ground.

Why did the banana go out with a prune?

Because it couldn't get a date.

Why did the banana cross the road?

It was running away from the monkey.

Traci: Why do elephants paint their faces yellow?

Stacy: I don't know, why?

Traci: So they can hide in banana trees.

Stacy: That's silly! I've never seen an elephant in a banana tree.

Traci: See! It works!

What do you call a banana with wings?

A fruit fly.

What's the opposite of a gorilla?

A stop-rilla.

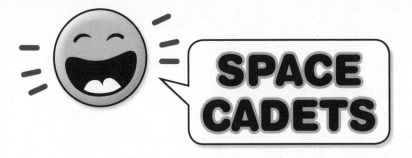

SPACE CADETS

What do you get when you cross an alien with a hot drink?

Gravi-tea.

Astronaut: Captain, we're going faster than the speed of sound.

Captain: What did you say?

Why should you never insult a Martian?

It might get its feelers hurt.

What's the center of gravity?

The letter "v."

What do you do with a green alien?

Wait until he ripens.

Why didn't Little Bo Peep fly to Mars?

She couldn't find her space-sheep.

What did the mouse pilot say to the shuttle passengers?

"This is your captain squeaking!"

If Martians live on Mars and Venusians live on Venus, what lives on Pluto?

Fleas!

Where do astronauts get their degrees?

From a mooniversity.

Favorite do-it-yourself book: *Space Travel* by Bill Jerome Rocket

How do you tie your shoes in outer space?

With an astro-knot.

Which planet has the most cows?

The mooooon.

Why did the shuttle pilot refuse to take flying lessons?

It was a crash course.

Why did the astronaut let go of her sundae?

She wanted an ice-cream float.

Where do you find black holes?
In black socks.

Why can't astronauts keep jobs?
They always get fired after training.

What do you get when you cross a chicken with an alien?
An eggstra-terrestrial.

What is a Jedi's favorite snack?
Obi-Wan Cannoli.

Why don't aliens celebrate birthdays?
They don't want to give away their presence.

What did the astronaut say when she walked into the space shuttle?
"Ouch!"

How many letters are in the alphabet?
Twenty-four...because E.T. went home.

Why haven't astronauts visited Mars?
They haven't been invited.

What do the planets get after orbiting the sun all day?

Dizzy.

How do you wash a space shuttle?

Fly it through a meteor shower.

Favorite tabloid tale: *I Saw an Alien* **by Omar Goodness**

Why did the alien abduct a dachshund?

It wanted a down-to-Earth pet.

Besides shooting stars, which other stars have tails?

Dory, Tigger, and Bambi.

What do you call a wizard in space?

A flying sorcerer.

What do you call a robot that takes the longest route?

R2-Detour.

What is fast, loud, and crunchy?

A rocket chip.

DON'T BEE SILLY

Why do bees hum?
Because they don't know how to whistle.

Can bees fly in rain?
Only if they wear their yellow jackets.

Why don't bees play baseball?
They're always too bees-y.

Why do bees walk on the ceiling?
If they walked on the floor, someone might step on them.

Doctor, Doctor! I keep seeing bees circling my head!
Don't worry. It's just a bug that's going around.

What's black and yellow and goes *zzub, zzub*?
A bee flying backward.

DON'T BEE SILLY!

Why is the letter "A" like a flower?
Because a bee always comes after it.

How do you know bees are happy?
They hum while they work.

Why do bees have sticky hair?
Because they use honeycombs.

What did the bee order at the fast-food joint?
A hum-burger.

Who's a bee's favorite composer?
Bee-thoven.

What did the bee in the sauna say?
"'Swarm in here!"

What was the bee's favorite musical?
Stinging in the Rain.

What is a bee's favorite sport?
Rug-bee.

Book buzz: *Looking at Bees* **by Amos Skeeto.**

What do you get when you cross a skunk with a bee?

You get stung by a stinker.

What do you call a wasp?

A wanna-bee.

Where do you take a wasp with a broken wing?

The waspital.

How do bees get to school?

They take the buzz.

What do you call a bee having a bad hair day?

A frizz-bee.

What comes after an April bee?

A May-bee.

What's black and yellow and flies above the clouds?

A bee in an airplane.

What's worse than being a fool?

Fooling with a bee!

What kind of wasp can you wear?

A yellow jacket.

DON'T BEE SILLY!

Who writes books for little bees?

Bee-trix Potter.

What buzzes and is wanted by the FBI?

A killer bee.

How does a bee cut firewood?

With a buzz saw.

What do you get when you cross a sheep with a bee?

A baaaa-humbug.

Girl: I'd like to buy a bee.

Pet store owner: We don't sell bees.

Girl: Then why do you have one in your front window?

Which insect can't play football?

The fumble-bee.

What kind of suit does a bee wear to work?

A buzz-ness suit.

Why did the bee go to the doctor?

It had hives.

What did the rose say to the bee?
"Buzz off!"

Which insect gets the best grade in English?
The spelling bee.

What does a bee sit on?
Its bee-hind.

What did the robber say to the bee?
"Your honey or your life."

What kind of phones do bees use?
Cell phones.

Where do bees go on vacation?
Stingapore.

SCARED SILLY

What happened when the werewolf swallowed the clock?

He got ticks.

Why wouldn't the vampire climb into his coffin at sunrise?

He was an all-day sucker.

What are a zombie's least favorite letters?

D K (decay).

Where does Medusa go when she visits Arizona?

The Petrified Forest.

Why won't Bigfoot cross the road?

Because that's what chickens do.

Do mummies like to visit King Tut's tomb?

Naw...they wouldn't be caught dead there.

Who's the best dancer at the monster ball?

The Boogieman.

What did one zombie say to the other zombie?

"Get a life!"

What does the Loch Ness monster eat for breakfast?

Bagels and lochs.

Why do vampire bats use red markers?

They like to draw blood.

What kind of monster is never around when you need him?

A wherewolf.

Where do mummies go for pizza?

Pizza Tut.

Why didn't the zombie lose its teeth?

It used toothpaste.

Why did King Kong climb the Empire State Building so quickly?

He had a plane to catch.

Which artist has the most haunted paintings?

Vincent van Ghost.

How many vampires does it take to change a lightbulb?

None. They prefer the dark.

What kind of key opens a casket?

A skeleton key.

Why did Batman go to the pet store?

To buy a Robin.

How does Dracula like his coffee?

De-coffin-ated.

Which three letters terrify the Invisible Man?

I-C-U.

What does Frankenstein do first thing every morning?

He wakes up.

Why does Bigfoot always leave behind footprints?

Because they're dirty.

Why do dragons love knights?
Because they're crunchy and good with ketchup.

What do you call two witches who share an apartment?
Broom-mates.

What did the mommy ghost say to the baby ghost?
"Don't spook until you're spooken to."

How did the zombie feel after partying all night?
Dead on his feet.

What is King Kong's favorite sandwich?
Go-rilla cheese.

How does a witch tell time?
With a witch watch.

Why doesn't the mummy take a vacation?
Because if he relaxes too much, he'll unwind.

Why did Dracula run around his coffin?
To catch up on his sleep.

Where do ghosts like to swim?
The Dead Sea.

What was the pirate's favorite fish?

The swordfish.

Where do vampires keep their money?

In blood banks.

How could the mummy have a brother if the mummy's brother had no brothers?

The mummy is a woman.

Why did the wolfman scratch himself?

No one else knew where he itched.

Why didn't the skeleton kid like to go to school?

Her heart wasn't in it.

When is it bad luck to have a black cat cross your path?

When you're a mouse.

How did the Phantom of the Opera get out of a locked room?

He played the piano until he found the right key.

What is Dracula's favorite fast food?

Fangfurters.

What has two arms, two wings, three heads, and eight legs?

A man riding a horse holding a chicken.

Where did the Headless Horseman find his head?

In the last place he looked.

Who's the clumsiest monster?

Clodzilla.

Why was the photographer arrested?

Because he shot people and then blew them up.

Why did Godzilla wrap a long string around a Japanese city?

He wanted a Tokyo-yo.

Why do zombies dine at the fanciest restaurants?

They only eat gore-met food.

Is Ghostland a country?

No. It's a terror-tory.

Why did Bigfoot Jr. shave off all his hair?

He wanted to be a little bare (bear).

SCARED SILLY

What's the first thing ghosts do when they get into a car?

They boo-ckle up.

What is a sea monster's favorite lunch?

A submarine sandwich.

Why do witches fly on broomsticks?

They're too lazy to walk.

What do you call a zombie track team?

The Running Dead.

What's a cannibal's favorite pizza?

Cheese, with everyone on it.

What is sweet, brown, and deadly?

Shark-infested chocolate pudding.

What was the baby zombie's favorite toy?

Its heady bear.

Who makes wishes come true for a witch?

A Feary Godmother.

Why did the haunted house hurt?

Because of all its window panes (pains).

EXTRA WACKY

Why couldn't Cinderella go to King Neptune's ball?
She didn't have a ferry godmother.

What is round and has a bad temper?
A vicious circle.

What should you do if you break your arm in two places?
Stay away from those places.

What is Tigger's favorite hot dog?
Wienie the Pooh.

Patient: My ear's ringing. What should I do?
Doctor: Answer it.

What is a pig's favorite fairy tale?
Slopping Beauty.

Which animals are best at multiplication?
Rabbits.

What happened when the king's men told Humpty Dumpty a joke?

He fell for it.

Teacher: What is 5Q + 5Q?

Student: 10Q.

Teacher: You're welcome!

Painful reading: *The Patient with the Exploding Bottom* by Stan Wellback

What do you call a boomerang that doesn't come back to you?

A bummerang.

How many skunks does it take to make a big stink?

A phew.

Why is lava red and hot?

Because if it were white and cold, it would be snow.

Did you know it takes three sheep to make one sweater?

I didn't even know they could knit!

What speaks every language?

An echo.

What do you get if you cross a dog with a chicken?

A pooched egg.

What did the skunk say when the wind changed?

"It all comes back to me now."

Why are barns so noisy?

The cows have horns.

Rooster #1 laid 3 eggs.
Rooster #2 laid 4 eggs.
How many eggs do you have?

None. Roosters don't lay eggs.

What do you call a small billy goat?

A peanut butter.

Where can you find an ocean with no water?

On a map.

When is a worm safe from the early bird?

When it sleeps late.

What is 11 + 2 + 4 - 17?

A lot of work for nothing!

What do you call a boy with a car on his head?
Jack.

Patient: Doctor, Doctor! My nose is running.
Doctor: No. I think it's not.

Did you hear about the clothesline robbery?
The underwear was held up by two clothespins.

What do you call a three-footed aardvark?
A yard-vark.

What did the bear cub say when his friend came to visit?
"I'd like you to meet my den mother."

Why did Miss Muffet need a map?
Because she lost her whey.

What kind of paper makes the best kites?
Flypaper.

Zach: Josh is whispering in class.
Teacher: Why does that bother you?
Zach: I can't hear what he's saying.

Why did Captain Hook cross the road?

To get to the secondhand shop.

What do you call a tuba's father?

Ooom-papa.

How many bugs can you put in an empty pint jar?

One. After that, it's not empty.

What's the best brain food?

Noodle soup.

Why did the math teacher skip the chapter on circles?

They were pointless.

What happened when 19 and 20 got into a fight?

Twenty-won.

What makes kindergarten teachers so good?

They know how to make the little things count.

What sits on the ocean bottom and shakes?

A nervous wreck.

What's green and goes camping?

A brussels scout.

Stinkiest book: *Too Many Beans* by Wynn D. Bottom

What's pink and fluffy?
Pink fluff.

What's blue and pink and fluffy?
Pink fluff holding its breath.

What did one potato chip say to the other?
"Let's go for a dip!"

How do little shellfish travel?
By taxi crab.

Why did the driver hold his nose?
His car had gas.

What kind of pliers do you use in math?
Multipliers.

How much dirt is in a hole with a three-foot circumference?
None. Holes are empty.

Which cowboy lives in the ocean?
Billy the Squid.

THE WACKIEST JOKES EVER!

Why are monsters large and hairy?

Because if they were small and hairless, they'd be rocks.

Who's the smallest king?

Henry the 1/8th.

What do you call a man who has no nose and no body?

Nobody nose!

What do you say if you have nut allergies?

Cashew!

Why can't bad actors go fishing?

They forget their lines.

Have you ever been to Prague? It's beautiful.

Definitely Czech it out.

What football player smells the best?

The scenter.

I ordered a joke book last week.

I didn't get it.

How do dragons learn to fly?

They just wing it.

Why do people like maple and cherry furniture?

Because carpenters don't make vanilla or strawberry.

2 THE FUNNIEST KNOCK-KNOCK JOKES EVER!

KNOCK-NAMES

Knock-knock!
Who's there?
Doris.
Doris who?
Doris open.
Can I come in?

Knock-knock!
Who's there?
Fanny.
Fanny who?
Fanny-body knocks,
I'm not home.

Knock-knock!
Who's there?
Athena.
Athena who?
Athena
flying saucer!

Knock-knock!
Who's there?
Emerson.
Emerson who?
Emerson
nice sneakers
you're wearing.

Knock-knock!
Who's there?
Hannah.
Hannah who?
Hannah partridge
in a pear tree.

Knock-knock!
Who's there?
Sancho.
Sancho who?
Sancho an email
but you
never answered.

Knock-knock!
Who's there?
Lionel.
Lionel who?
Lionel bite you if you stick your head in its mouth.

Knock-knock!
Who's there?
Howell.
Howell who?
Howell you find out if you don't open the door?

Knock-knock!
Who's there?
José.
José who?
José can you see...

Knock-knock!
Who's there?
Kent.
Kent who?
Kent you see for yourself?

Knock-knock!
Who's there?
Gus.
Gus who?
That's what *you're* supposed to do!

Knock-knock!
Who's there?
Eliza.
Eliza who?
Eliza lot so don't trust 'im.

Knock-knock!
Who's there?
Carmen.
Carmen who?
Carmen get it!

Knock-knock!
Who's there?
Howard.
Howard who?
Howard I know?

Knock-knock!
Who's there?
Freddy.
Freddy who?
Freddy or not,
here I come!

Knock-knock!
Who's there?
Celeste.
Celeste who?
Celeste time I
knock on *your* door.

Knock-knock!
Who's there?
Kim.
Kim who?
Kim too late for
the party.

Knock-knock!
Who's there?
Olive.
Olive who?
Olive here,
let me in!

Knock-knock!
Who's there?
Imus.
Imus who?
Imus be outta
my mind.

Knock-knock!
Who's there?
Sarah.
Sarah who?
Sarah echo
in here?

Knock-knock!
Who's there?
Albie.
Albie who?
Albie glad when
you finally
let me in.

Knock-knock!
Who's there?
Gladys.
Gladys who?
Gladys not snowing.

Knock-knock!
Who's there?
Ida.
Ida who?
Ida know...sorry.

Knock-knock!
Who's there?
Darren.
Darren who?
Darren you
to open the door.

Knock-knock!
Who's there?
Wynn.
Wynn who?
Wynn a few,
lose a few.

Knock-knock!
Who's there?
Claire.
Claire who?
Claire the way!
I'm comin' through.

Knock-knock!
Who's there?
Tyrone.
Tyrone who?
Tyrone shoelaces.

Knock-knock!
Who's there?
Isabel.
Isabel who?
Isabel ringing or
am I going nuts?

Knock-knock!
Who's there?
Anita.
Anita who?
Anita use the toilet.

Knock-knock!
Who's there?
Nadya.
Nadya who?
Nadya head if
you understand
this joke.

DOC KNOCKS

Doc-Doc!
Who's there?
Esther.
Esther who?
Esther a doctor in the house?

Doc-Doc!
Who's there?
Czar.
Czar who?
Czar a different doctor in the house?

Doc-Doc!
Who's there?
Gargoyle.
Gargoyle who?
Gargoyle with salt water for a sore throat.

Doc-Doc!
Who's there?
Watts.
Watts who?
Watts up, Doc?

Doc-Doc!
Who's there?
Venice.
Venice who?
Venice the last time you saw a doctor?

Doc-Doc!
Who's there?
Colin.
Colin who?
Colin the doctor, of course.

Doc-Doc!

Who's there?

A knock-knock joke with a cold.

Doc-Doc!

Who's there?

Otto.

Otto who?

Otto know, who are you?

Doc-Doc!

Who's there?

Denise.

Denise who?

Denise are above de ankles.

Doc-Doc!

Who's there?

Schick.

Schick who?

Schick as a dog.

Doc-Doc!

Who's there?

Genoa.

Genoa who?

Genoa good dentist?

Doc-Doc!

Who's there?

Vicki.

Vicki who?

Vicki to good health is a healthy diet.

Doc-Doc!

Who's there?

Henrietta.

Henrietta who?

Henrietta worm that was in his apple.

Doc-Doc!

Who's there?

Dublin.

Dublin who?

Dublin over in pain from all these knock-knock jokes.

Doc-Doc!

Who's there?

Mia.

Mia who?

Mia stomach is killing
me from laughing.

Doc-Doc!

Who's there?

Kenya.

Kenya who?

Kenya call
the doctor, please?

Doc-Doc!

Who's there?

Goliath.

Goliath who?

Goliath down,
you look sick.

Doc-Doc!

Who's there?

Dispense.

Dispense who?

Dispense are
too tight.
I must have
gained weight.

Doc-Doc!

Who's there?

Iota.

Iota who?

Iota send you to
the hospital.

Doc-Doc!

Who's there?

Disease.

Disease who?

Disease the worst
disaster I've ever seen.

Doc-Doc!

Who's there?

Morrie.

Morrie who?

Morrie tells
knock-knock jokes,
the sicker I feel.

Doc-Doc!

Who's there?

Eileen.

Eileen who?

Eileen on a crutch
because I broke
my foot.

Doc-Doc!

Who's there?

Concha.

Concha who?

Concha get rid of these chicken pox?

Doc-Doc!

Who's there?

Hatch.

Hatch who?

I'll come back when you stop sneezing.

Doc-Doc!

Who's there?

Oldest.

Oldest who?

Oldest knocking has bruised my knuckles.

Doc-Doc!

Who's there?

Goose.

Goose who?

Goose see a doctor for that cough.

Doc-Doc!

Who's there?

Ada.

Ada who?

Ada whole box of chocolates and now I'm sick.

Doc-Doc!

Who's there?

Issue.

Issue who?

Issue the doctor?

Doc-Doc!

Who's there?

Althea.

Althea who?

Althea next time.

Doc-Doc!

Who's there?

Nita.

Nita who?

Nita cure for all these knock-knock jokes.

Doc-Doc!
Who's there?
Moose.
Moose who?
Moose have been something I ate.

Doc-Doc!
Who's there?
Moustache.
Moustache who?
Moustache you to stop telling knock-knock jokes.

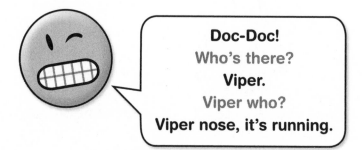

Doc-Doc!
Who's there?
Viper.
Viper who?
Viper nose, it's running.

KNOCK 'EM COWBOY!

Knock-knock!
Who's there?
Yah.
Yah who?
Ride 'em,
cowboy!

Knock-knock!
Who's there?
Tick.
Tick who?
Tick 'em up!
This is a robbery.

Knock-knock!
Who's there?
Despair.
Despair who?
Despair of cowboy
boots is too tight.

Knock-knock!
Who's there?
Orange.
Orange who?
Orange you
Billy the Kid?

Knock-knock!
Who's there?
Cattle.
Cattle who?
Cattle purr
if you pet her.

Knock-knock!
Who's there?
July.
July who?
July awake
at night
counting sheep?

Knock-knock!
Who's there?
Pasture.
Pasture who?
Pasture bedtime,
cowpoke!

Knock-knock!
Who's there?
Beecher.
Beecher who?
Beecher to
the draw again.

Knock-knock!
Who's there?
Dewey.
Dewey who?
Dewey have any
more beef jerky?

Knock-knock!
Who's there?
Alma Gibbons.
Alma Gibbons who?
Alma Gibbons you
twenty-four hours
to get out of town.

Knock-knock!
Who's there?
Mustang.
Mustang who?
Mustang up
the phone.
Chow's on.

Knock-knock!
Who's there?
Event.
Event who?
Event thataway!

Knock-knock!
Who's there?
Russell.
Russell who?
Russell up
some grub!

Knock-knock!
Who's there?
Mike Howe.
Mike Howe who?
Mike Howe is sick.
Gotta call the vet.

Knock-knock!
Who's there?
Lass.
Lass who?
Lass-o that cow
if you can.

Knock-knock!
Who's there?
Orson.
Orson who?
Orson
around again?

Knock-knock!
Who's there?
Agate.
Agate who?
Agate you
covered, outlaw!

Knock-knock!
Who's there?
Icon.
Icon who?
Icon hardly wait
to get back to
my bunk.

Knock-knock!
Who's there?
Sonya.
Sonya who?
Sonya foot? I can
smell it from here.

Knock-knock!
Who's there?
Danged Bob Dwyer.
Danged Bob
Dwyer who?
Danged Bob Dwyer
ripped my
pants again.

Knock-knock!
Who's there?
Gideon.
Gideon who?
Gideon your horse
and giddyup.

Knock-knock!
Who's there?
Calder.
Calder who?
Calder sheriff!
I've been robbed.

Knock-knock!
Who's there?
Owl.
Owl who?
Owl aboard,
the train is leaving.

Knock-knock!
Who's there?
European.
European who?
European all over
my favorite boots.

Knock-knock!
Who's there?
Barbara.
Barbara who?
Barbara black sheep,
have you any wool?

Knock-knock!
Who's there?
Yah.
Yah who?
I'm glad to see
you too, pardner.

Knock-knock!
Who's there?
Robin.
Robin who?
Robin banks is no
way to make a living.

Knock-knock!
Who's there?
Sawyer.
Sawyer who?
Sawyer picture on
a wanted poster.

Knock-knock!
Who's there?
Arizona.
Arizona who?
Arizona room for one
of us in this town.

Knock-knock!
Who's there?
Manuel.
Manuel who?
Manuel be sorry
if you don't open
this door!

WHO'S KNOCKING?

Knock-knock!
Who's there?
Yah.
Yah who?
**No thanks,
I prefer Google.**

Knock-knock!
Who's there?
Abe Lincoln.
Abe Lincoln who?
**Wait! You don't
know who
Abe Lincoln is?**

Knock-knock!
Who's there?
Omelet.
Omelet who?
**Omelet smarter
than you think!**

Knock-knock!
Who's there?
Canoe.
Canoe who?
**Canoe loan
me $20?**

Knock-knock!
Who's there?
Dozen.
Dozen who?
**Dozen anybody
know how to
answer a door?**

Knock-knock!
Who's there?
Rover.
Rover who?
**It's all Rover
between us.**

Knock-knock!
Who's there?
Bitter.
Bitter who?
**Bitter watch
your step.**

Knock-knock!
Who's there?
Fido.
Fido who?
**Fido I always
have to knock?**

Knock-knock!
Who's there?
Midas.
Midas who?
**Midas well
open up.**

Knock-knock!
Who's there?
Wooden shoe.
Wooden shoe who?
**Wooden shoe
like to know!**

Knock-knock!
Who's there?
Eva.
Eva who?
**Eva told you,
would you let me in?**

Knock-knock!
Who's there?
Acid.
Acid who?
Acid let me in!

Knock-knock!
Who's there?
Huron.
Huron who?
Huron on my foot!

Knock-knock!
Who's there?
Turnip.
Turnip who?
**Turnip the heat,
it's freezing
in here!**

Knock-knock!
Who's there?
Boise.
Boise who?
Boise a sore loser!

Knock-knock!
Who's there?
Jamaica.
Jamaica who?
Jamaica me
a chocolate cake?

Knock-knock!
Who's there?
Pencil.
Pencil who?
Your pencil fall
down with no belt.

Knock-knock!
Who's there?
Ether.
Ether who?
Ether Bunny.

Knock-knock!
Who's there?
Samoa.
Samoa who?
Samoa
Ether Bunnies.

Knock-knock!
Who's there?
Toad.
Toad who?
Toad you before
but you forgot.

Knock-knock!
Who's there?
Lass.
Lass who?
Lass one in
is a rotten egg.

Knock-knock!
Who's there?
Irish.
Irish who?
Irish you a merry
Christmas and
a happy New Year.

Knock-knock!
Who's there?
Bacon.
Bacon who?
I'm bacon a cake
for your birthday.

Knock-knock!
Who's there?
Ach.
Ach who?
Gesundheit!

Knock-knock!
Who's there?
Chicken.
Chicken who?
Chicken to see if
you're awake.

Knock-knock!
Who's there?
Ferry.
Ferry who?
Ferry funny,
now let me in!

Knock-knock!
Who's there?
Willa.
Willa who?
Willa stop it with
the corny
knock-knock jokes?

Knock-knock!
Who's there?
Juicy.
Juicy who?
Juicy anyone
else out here?

Knock-knock!
Who's there?
Shoes.
Shoes who?
Shoes me.
Can I be excused?

Knock-knock!
Who's there?
Major.
Major who?
Major ask,
didn't I?

Knock-knock!
Who's there?
Vilify.
Vilify who?
Vilify knew my name,
I would tell you.

Knock-knock!
Who's there?
Zagat.
Zagat who?
Zagat in the Hat!

Knock-knock!
Who's there?
Goldilocks.
Goldilocks who?
Goldilocks herself
out of the house
all the time.

Knock-knock!
Who's there?
Papaya.
Papaya who?
Papaya
the sailor man.

Knock-knock!
Who's there?
Byron.
Byron who?
Byron, get one free.

Knock-knock!
Who's there?
Cod.
Cod who?
Cod you red-handed
with the loot!

Knock-knock!
Who's there?
Llama.
Llama who?
Llama so glad
to see you.

Knock-knock!
Who's there?
Dewey.
Dewey who?
Dewey have any garlic?
Dracula's at
the door.

KNEE KNOCKS

Knock-knock!
Who's there?
Yeti.
Yeti who?
Yeti 'nother
knock-knock joke.

Knock-knock!
Who's there?
Yule.
Yule who?
Open this door or
yule be sorry.

Knock-knock!
Who's there?
Howl.
Howl who?
Howl you
know unless you
open the door?

Knock-knock!
Who's there?
Hugo.
Hugo who?
Hugo first,
I'm scared.

Knock-knock!
Who's there?
Freda.
Freda who?
Freda letting me in,
aren't you?

Knock-knock!
Who's there?
Fangs.
Fangs who?
Fangs for opening
the door.
Bwah-ha-ha!

Knock-knock!
Who's there?
Jess.
Jess who?
Jess me and
my shadow.

Knock-knock!
Who's there?
Barry.
Barry who?
Barry my bones in
the graveyard.

Knock-knock!
Who's there?
Thumping.
Thumping who?
Thumping green
and thlimy ith
crawling up your leg!

Knock-knock!
Who's there?
Leaf.
Leaf who?
Leaf me alone!

Knock-knock!
Who's there?
Wash out.
Wash out who?
Wash out for
the zombies!

Knock-knock!
Who's there?
Ivor.
Ivor who?
Ivor let me in or
I'll blow
your house down.

Knock-knock!
Who's there?
Gruesome.
Gruesome who?
Gruesome much
my clothes don't fit.

Knock-knock!
Who's there?
Mustard bean.
Mustard bean who?
Mustard bean
a surprise to find
Bigfoot at your door.

Knock-knock!
Who's there?
Ice cream.
Ice cream who?
Ice cream every time
I see your face.

Knock-knock!
Who's there?
Witches.
Witches who?
Witches
the way home?

Knock-knock!
Who's there?
Hoosier.
Hoosier who?
Hoosier 'fraid of
the Big Bad Wolf?

Knock-knock!
Who's there?
Flea.
Flea who?
Flea while you can!

Knock-knock!
Who's there?
Cinnamon.
Cinnamon who?
Cinnamonster,
bolt the door!

Knock-knock!
Who's there?
Ding-dong.
Ding-dong who?
"Ding-dong,
the witch is dead."

Knock-knock!
Who's there?
Ooze.
Ooze who?
Ooze going
to open the door?

Knock-knock!
Who's there?
Diesel.
Diesel who?
Diesel be
your last chance
to let me in!

Knock-knock!
Who's there?
Philip.
Philip who?
Philip this bag with treats, please.

Knock-knock!
Who's there?
Donatello.
Donatello who?
Donatello anyone— I'm a werewolf.

Knock-knock!
Who's there?
Keith.
Keith who?
Keith me! I want to be a prince again.

Knock-knock!
Who's there?
Ivan.
Ivan who?
Ivan to drink your blood.

Knock-knock!
Who's there?
Deluxe.
Deluxe who?
Deluxe Ness Monster.

Knock-knock!
Who's there?
Lucretia.
Lucretia who?
Lucretia from the Black Lagoon.

Knock-knock!
Who's there?
Frank N.
Frank N. who?
Frank N. Stein.

Knock-knock!
Who's there?
Hallways.
Hallways who?
Hallways knew you were a vampire.

Knock-knock!
Who's there?
Mohair.
Mohair who?
There's mohair
on your wart than
on your head.

Knock-knock!
Who's there?
Dutch.
Dutch who?
Dutch me and
I'll scream!

Knock-knock!
Who's there?
Spell.
Spell who?
W-H-O.

Knock-knock!
Who's there?
Aida.
Aida who?
Aida whole village
and now I'm
gonna eat you.

Knock-knock!
Who's there?
Icy.
Icy who?
Icy a monster
under your bed.

Knock-knock!
Who's there?
Sadie.
Sadie who?
Sadie magic word
and I'll let you in.

Knock-knock!
Who's there?
Needle.
Needle who?
Needle little
help getting away
from Godzilla.

Knock-knock!
Who's there?
Vino.
Vino who?
Vino how to
make you talk.

KNOCK AROUND THE HOUSE

Knock-knock!
Who's there?
Norma Lee.
Norma Lee who?
Norma Lee I'd ring
the doorbell.

Knock-knock!
Who's there?
Chicken.
Chicken who?
Chicken your
pocket. I think
your key's in there.

Knock-knock!
Who's there?
Pasta.
Pasta who?
Pasta bread,
I'm hungry.

Knock-knock!
Who's there?
Arthur.
Arthur who?
Arthur any
brownies left?

Knock-knock!
Who's there?
Bean.
Bean who?
Bean a long time
since breakfast.

Knock-knock!
Who's there?
Eyewash.
Eyewash who?
Eyewash
the dishes, you dry.

Knock-knock!
Who's there?
Alma.
Alma who?
Alma cookies
are gone!

Knock-knock!
Who's there?
Dwayne.
Dwayne who?
Dwayne the
bathtub,
I'm dwowning.

Knock-knock!
Who's there?
Ammonia.
Ammonia who?
Ammonia a little kid.
Let me in!

Knock-knock!
Who's there?
House.
House who?
House about
opening this door?

Knock-knock!
Who's there?
Lego.
Lego who?
Lego of
the door handle!

Knock-knock!
Who's there?
Dishes.
Dishes who?
Dishes me, silly!

Knock-knock!
Who's there?
Butternut.
Butternut who?
Butternut go
outside,
it's raining.

Knock-knock!
Who's there?
Tuba.
Tuba who?
Tuba toothpaste.

Knock-knock!
Who's there?
Megan.
Megan who?
Megan apple pie
for dessert.

Knock-knock!
Who's there?
Ivana.
Ivana who?
Ivana go
to Disneyland.

Knock-knock!
Who's there?
Pizza.
Pizza who?
Pizza chocolate cake
would be good.

Knock-knock!
Who's there?
Dismay.
Dismay who?
Dismay be the last
time I come
to *your* house.

Knock-knock!
Who's there?
Needle.
Needle who?
Needle little snack.

Knock-knock!
Who's there?
Hominy.
Hominy who?
Hominy times do I
have to knock?

Knock-knock!
Who's there?
Window.
Window who?
Window we
get to play
something else?

Knock-knock!
Who's there?
Psalm.
Psalm who?
Psalm day I'm
going to get
my own room.

Knock-knock!
Who's there?
Beets.
Beets who?
Beets me, I can't
even remember
my name.

Knock-knock!
Who's there?
Alcott.
Alcott who?
Alcott the cake,
you pour the milk.

Knock-knock!
Who's there?
Peas.
Peas who?
Peas pass the milk.

Knock-knock!
Who's there?
Belladonna.
Belladonna who?
Belladonna work so
I had to knock.

Knock-knock!
Who's there?
Eton.
Eton who?
Eton out of
the garbage is gross!

Knock-knock!
Who's there?
Cash.
Cash who?
No thanks,
I'm allergic to nuts.

Knock-knock!
Who's there?
Goat.
Goat who?
Goat to your room
right now!

Knock-knock!
Who's there?
Hewlett.
Hewlett who?
Hewlett
the dogs out?

Knock-knock!
Who's there?
Egg roll.
Egg roll who?
Egg roll off the table
and broke.

Knock-knock!
Who's there?
Sausage.
Sausage who?
I never sausage
a mess!

Knock-knock!
Who's there?
Dryer.
Dryer who?
Dryer you trying to get
into my house?

Knock-knock!
Who's there?
Justice.
Justice who?
Justice I suspected—
you stole the pie!

Knock-knock!
Who's there?
Emmett.
Emmett who?
Emmett
the back door,
not the front.

Knock-knock!
Who's there?
Queen.
Queen who?
Queen up
your room.

Knock-knock!
Who's there?
Clothesline.
Clothesline who?
Clothesline all over
the floor.
What a mess!

CAMP KNOCK-KNOCK

Knock-knock!
Who's there?
Intense.
Intense who?
Intense is where scouts sleep.

Knock-knock!
Who's there?
Scott.
Scott who?
Scott to be bears in these woods.

Knock-knock!
Who's there?
Gnats.
Gnats who?
Gnats the way the cookie crumbles

Knock-knock!
Who's there?
Beehive.
Beehive who?
Beehive yourself or else!

Knock-knock!
Who's there?
Cook.
Cook who?
Yes.
Yes, you are.

Knock-knock!
Who's there?
Itch.
Itch who?
Itch a long way to camp.

Knock-knock!
Who's there?
Donalette.
Donalette who?
Donalette
the bedbugs bite.

Knock-knock!
Who's there?
Spider.
Spider who?
In spider
everything, you're
my best friend.

Knock-knock!
Who's there?
Bee.
Bee who?
Bee nice and
build a fire.

Knock-knock!
Who's there?
Esther.
Esther who?
Esther a scorpion in
your sleeping bag?

Knock-knock!
Who's there?
Roach.
Roach who?
Roach you a letter
from camp.

Knock-knock!
Who's there?
Antson.
Antson who?
Antson my pants make
me do a dance.

Knock-knock!
Who's there?
A pile-up.
A pile-up who?
A pile-up poo
attracts flies.

Knock-knock!
Who's there?
Edward B.
Edward B. who?
Edward B. nice
if you cleaned
the cabin.

Knock-knock!
Who's there?
Zombies.
Zombies who?
Zombies just flew
in the tent.

Knock-knock!
Who's there?
Wren.
Wren who?
Wren it rains,
it pours.

Knock-knock!
Who's there?
Oliver.
Oliver who?
Oliver clothes got
soaked in the rain.

Knock-knock!
Who's there?
Water.
Water who?
Water you doing up
after lights out?

Knock-knock!
Who's there?
Achilles.
Achilles who?
Achilles mosquitoes
if they don't stop
biting me.

Knock-knock!
Who's there?
Sparrow.
Sparrow who?
Sparrow me
the details.

Knock-knock!
Who's there?
Ken.
Ken who?
Ken you hear
something growling?

Knock-knock!
Who's there?
Quack.
Quack who?
Quack another joke
and I'm outta here.

Knock-knock!
Who's there?
Dawn.
Dawn who?
**Dawn wake me
up so early.**

Knock-knock!
Who's there?
Toucan.
Toucan who?
**Toucan play
this game.**

Knock-knock!
Who's there?
Arthur.
Arthur who?
**Arthur any snakes
in this tent?**

Knock-knock!
Who's there?
Wire.
Wire who?
**Wire you eating
that bug?**

Knock-knock!
Who's there?
Hive.
Hive who?
**Hive been workin'
on the railroad.**

Knock-knock!
Who's there?
Jethro.
Jethro who?
**Jethro, ro, ro
your boat...**

Knock-knock!
Who's there?
Butternut.
Butternut who?
**Butternut snore
too loud.**

Knock-knock!
Who's there?
Bat.
Bat who?
**Bat you
can't guess!**

Knock-knock!
Who's there?
Hawk.
Hawk who?
Hawk...
who goes there?

Knock-knock!
Who's there?
Romeo.
Romeo who?
Romeover to
the other side of
the lake and I'll tell you.

Knock-knock!
Who's there?
Spain.
Spain who?
Spain to be bitten
by a horsefly.

Knock-knock!
Who's there?
Formosa.
Formosa who?
Formosa my life
I've been
allergic to bees.

Knock-knock!
Who's there?
Argo.
Argo who?
Argo fly a kite!

Knock-knock!
Who's there?
Bug spray.
Bug spray who?
Bug spray they won't
get squished.

Knock-knock!
Who's there?
Mint.
Mint who?
Mint to tell you about
that hornet's nest.

Knock-knock!
Who's there?
Oily.
Oily who?
The oily bird
catches the worm.

Knock-knock!
Who's there?
Weevil.
Weevil who?
Weevil go
swimming today.

Knock-knock!
Who's there?
Luke.
Luke who?
Luke out for
snapping turtles
in the lake

Knock-knock!
Who's there?
Outer.
Outer who?
Outer my way,
I'm comin' in!

Knock-knock!
Who's there?
Owls.
Owls who?
Owls well that
ends well.

Knock-knock!
Who's there?
Amy.
Amy who?
Amy-fraid of ghost stories.

WILDER KNOCKS

Knock-knock!
Who's there?
Detour.
Detour who?
**Detour of de zoo
starts in
five minutes.**

Knock-knock!
Who's there?
Weasel.
Weasel who?
**Weasel while
you work.**

Knock-knock!
Who's there?
Oink oink.
Oink oink who?
**Wow, a pig and owl
at the door!**

Knock-knock!
Who's there?
Walrus.
Walrus who?
**Walrus asking
silly questions,
aren't you?**

Knock-knock!
Who's there?
Goat.
Goat who?
**Goat to the door
and find out.**

Knock-knock!
Who's there?
Noah.
Noah who?
**Noah guy with an ark?
It's raining cats and
dogs out here.**

Knock-knock!
Who's there?
Anteater.
Anteater who?
Anteater dinner, but uncle didn't eat a thing.

Knock-knock!
Who's there?
Aurora.
Aurora who?
Aurora's coming from those bushes.

Knock-knock!
Who's there?
Celia.
Celia who?
Celia later, alligator.

Knock-knock!
Who's there?
Rhino.
Rhino who?
Rhino more knock-knock jokes than you do.

Knock-knock!
Who's there?
Wet.
Wet who?
Wet me in, it's raining.

Knock-knock!
Who's there?
Thistle.
Thistle who?
Thistle make you laugh.

Knock-knock!
Who's there?
Catsup.
Catsup who?
Catsup a tree! Call the fire department.

Knock-knock!
Who's there?
Lionel.
Lionel who?
Lionel eat you if you get too close.

Knock-knock!
Who's there?
Rook.
Rook who?
Rook out!
The sky is falling.

Knock-knock!
Who's there?
Ellie Fence.
Ellie Fence who?
Ellie Fence
love peanuts.

Knock-knock!
Who's there?
Viaduct.
Viaduct who?
Who knows
viaduct quacks?

Knock-knock!
Who's there?
Iguana.
Iguana who?
Iguana hold
your hand!

Knock-knock!
Who's there?
Arf.
Arf who?
Arf forgot.

Knock-knock!
Who's there?
Foreign.
Foreign who?
Foreign
20 blackbirds
baked in a pie.

Knock-knock!
Who's there?
Raisin.
Raisin who?
Raisin chickens
is hard work.

Knock-knock!
Who's there?
Howl.
Howl who?
Howl we get away
from all these
knock-knock jokes?

Knock-knock!
Who's there?
Zookeeper.
Zookeeper who?
Zookeeper away
from me.

Knock-knock!
Who's there?
Hewlett.
Hewlett who?
Hewlett
the monkeys
out of the cage?

Knock-knock!
Who's there?
Wendy Katz.
Wendy Katz who?
Wendy Katz away,
de mice will play.

Knock-knock!
Who's there?
Forest.
Forest who?
Forest the number
after three.

Knock-knock!
Who's there?
Detail.
Detail who?
Detail is
wagging de dog.

Knock-knock!
Who's there?
Wes Q.
Wes Q. who?
Wes Q. me from
the quicksand!

Knock-knock!
Who's there?
Claws.
Claws who?
Claws the door!
There's a
grizzly outside.

Knock-knock!
Who's there?
Hugh.
Hugh who?
Hugh can't stop
a charging rhino.

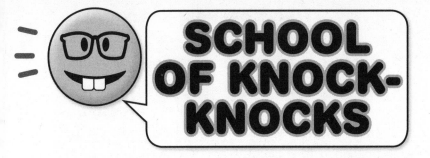

SCHOOL OF KNOCK-KNOCKS

Knock-knock!
Who's there?
Phineas.
Phineas who?
Phineas
thing happened at
school today.

Knock-knock!
Who's there?
Sid.
Sid who?
Sid down and get
to work!

Knock-knock!
Who's there?
Radio.
Radio who?
Radio not, here
I come!

Knock-knock!
Who's there?
Broken pencil.
Broken pencil who?
Forget it. This joke
is pointless.

Knock-knock!
Who's there?
Earl.
Earl who?
Earl be glad
when it's summer
vacation.

Knock-knock!
Who's there?
Zizi.
Zizi who?
Zizi to pass the test
when you study.

Knock-knock!
Who's there?
Dishwasher.
Dishwasher who?
Dishwasher last chance.
Go see the principal!

Knock-knock!
Who's there?
Jewel.
Jewel who?
Jewel be glad to
know I won
the spelling bee.

Knock-knock!
Who's there?
Norway.
Norway who?
Norway am I gonna
miss recess.

Knock-knock!
Who's there?
Viper.
Viper who?
Viper feet, you're
tracking mud in
the hall.

Knock-knock!
Who's there?
Avocado.
Avocado who?
Avocado cold so
I'm staying home.

Knock-knock!
Who's there?
Tennis.
Tennis who?
Tennis three
plus seven.

Knock-knock!
Who's there?
Oz.
Oz who?
Oz just about
to answer
that question.

Knock-knock!
Who's there?
Russian.
Russian who?
Russian around
because I'm late
for school.

Knock-knock!
Who's there?
Diesel.
Diesel who?
"Diesel man, he played one, he played knick-knack on a drum."

Knock-knock!
Who's there?
Auto.
Auto who?
Auto know the answer, but I forgot.

Knock-knock!
Who's there?
Mister.
Mister who?
Mister school bus again.

Knock-knock!
Who's there?
Juneau.
Juneau who?
Juneau the words to "The Star-Spangled Banner"?

Knock-knock!
Who's there?
Thermos.
Thermos who?
Thermos be some way out of doing all this homework.

Knock-knock!
Who's there?
Babylon.
Babylon who?
Babylon if you want, but I'm not listening.

Knock-knock!
Who's there?
Repeat.
Repeat who?
Who! Who!

Knock-knock!
Who's there?
Pecan.
Pecan who?
Pecan someone your own size.

Knock-knock!
Who's there?
F-2.
F-2 who?
Do I F-2 go
to school today?

Knock-knock!
Who's there?
Swatter.
Swatter who?
Swatter you doing
after school?

Knock-knock!
Who's there?
Danielle.
Danielle who?
Danielle at me,
I didn't do anything.

Knock-knock!
Who's there?
Ahab.
Ahab who?
Ahab to go
to the bathroom.

Knock-knock!
Who's there?
Censure.
Censure who?
Censure so
smart, you do
my homework.

Knock-knock!
Who's there?
Sam.
Sam who?
Sam old story.
How about a new one?

Knock-knock!
Who's there?
Gladys.
Gladys who?
Gladys Friday!

Knock-knock!
Who's there?
Adam.
Adam who?
Adam up and
tell me the total.

Knock-knock!
Who's there?
Sis.
Sis who?
Sis any way to treat your best friend?

Knock-knock!
Who's there?
Want.
Want who?
Good. Now try counting to three.

Knock-knock!
Who's there?
Giovanni.
Giovanni who?
Giovanni come out and play?

Knock-knock!
Who's there?
Chaos.
Chaos who?
Chaos the letter that comes after J.

Knock-knock!
Who's there?
Harris.
Harris who?
Harris your book report coming along?

Knock-knock!
Who's there?
Haiku.
Haiku who?
Haiku'd have danced all night!

Knock-knock!
Who's there?
Hair comb.
Hair comb who?
Hair comb the clowns.

Knock-knock!
Who's there?
I am.
I am who?
Oh, no! You forgot
who you are?

Knock-knock!
Who's there?
Disguise.
Disguise who?
Disguise are
where planes fly.

Knock-knock!
Who's there?
Pea.
Pea who?
Pea-u!
Something stinks.

Knock-knock!
Who's there?
Darby.
Darby who?
Darby a lot of
pirates in
these waters.

Knock-knock!
Who's there?
Eve.
Eve who?
Eve-ho,
me hearties!

Knock-knock!
Who's there?
Interrupting pirate.
Interrupting pirate wh—
Arrrrrh!

Knock-knock!
Who's there?
Water.
Water who?
**Water you doing
in my house?**

Knock-knock!
Who's there?
France.
France who?
**You know...France!
Where they make
French fries.**

Knock-knock!
Who's there?
Upton.
Upton who?
**Upton no good...
as usual.**

Knock-knock!
Who's there?
Gumby.
Gumby who?
**Gumby our guest
for dinner.**

Knock-knock!
Who's there?
Concha.
Concha who?
**Concha come out
and play?**

Knock-knock!
Who's there?
Icing.
Icing who?
**Icing off-key,
so cover your ears.**

Knock-knock!
Who's there?
Mikey.
Mikey who?
**Mikey won't work,
open the door!**

Knock-knock!
Who's there?
Maida.
Maida who?
Maida Force be with you!

Knock-knock!
Who's there?
Yoda.
Yoda who?
Yoda one who won't open da door.

Knock-knock!
Who's there?
Howard.
Howard who?
Howard you like to be outside while somebody asks, "Who's there?"

Knock-knock!
Who's there?
Ashley.
Ashley who?
Ashley, I changed my mind. I don't want to come in.

Knock-knock!
Who's there?
Turnip.
Turnip who?
Turnip the TV so I can hear it.

Knock-knock!
Who's there?
Winnie Thup.
Winnie Thup who?
And Tigger, too!

Knock-knock!
Who's there?
Mandy.
Mandy who?
Mandy lifeboats, we're sinking!

Knock-knock!
Who's there?
Butcher.
Butcher who?
Butcher right foot in, butcher right foot out...

Knock-knock!
Who's there?
Felix.
Felix who?
Felix my ice-cream
cone again,
he'll regret it.

Knock-knock!
Who's there?
Begonia.
Begonia who?
Begonia pardon,
could you get
off my foot?

Knock-knock!
Who's there?
Thumb.
Thumb who?
Thumb day my
printh will come.

Knock-knock!
Who's there?
Wire.
Wire who?
Wire you drinking
my hot chocolate?

Knock-knock!
Who's there?
Broccoli.
Broccoli who?
Don't be silly.
Broccoli doesn't
have a last name.

Knock-knock!
Who's there?
Letta.
Letta who?
Letta the
dog outside.

Knock-knock!
Who's there?
Urine.
Urine who?
Urine so
much trouble!

Knock-knock!
Who's there?
Muppet.
Muppet who?
Muppet up before
somebody slips in it.

Knock-knock!
Who's there?
Xavier.
Xavier who?
Xavier breath.

Knock-knock!
Who's there?
Stopwatch.
Stopwatch who?
Stopwatch you're
doing right now!

Knock-knock!
Who's there?
Utica.
Utica who?
Utica long way
home today.

Knock-knock!
Who's there?
Foster.
Foster who?
Foster than
a speeding bullet.

Knock-knock!
Who's there?
Erma.
Erma who?
"Erma little teapot,
short and stout..."

Knock-knock!
Who's there?
Candy.
Candy who?
Candy knock-knock
jokes stop now?

Knock-knock!
Who's there?
Dishes.
Dishes who?
Dishes the end
of the book.

Knock-knock!
Who's there?
Justin.
Justin who?
Justin the
neighborhood and
thought I'd come over.

Knock-knock!
Who's there?
Hummus.
Hummus who?
Hummus a tune...
because I don't
know the words.

Knock-knock!
Who's there?
Guitar.
Guitar who?
Guitar coats,
it's time to go.

Knock-knock!
Who's there?
Pasta.
Pasta who?
Pasta la vista, baby!

Knock-knock!
Who's there?
Icing.
Icing who?
Icing really loud.

Knock-knock!
Who's there?
Dr. Jacklyn.
Dr. Jacklyn who?
Dr. Jacklyn Mr. Hyde.

Knock-knock!
Who's there?
Eel.
Eel who?
Physician, eel thyself.

Knock-knock!
Who's there?
Control freak.
Cont—
Okay, now you
have to say,
"Control freak, who?"

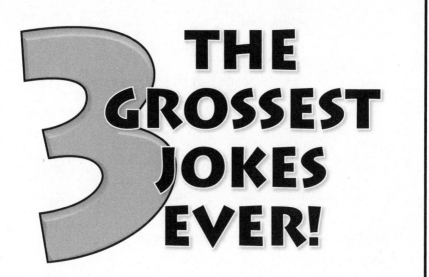

3 THE GROSSEST JOKES EVER!

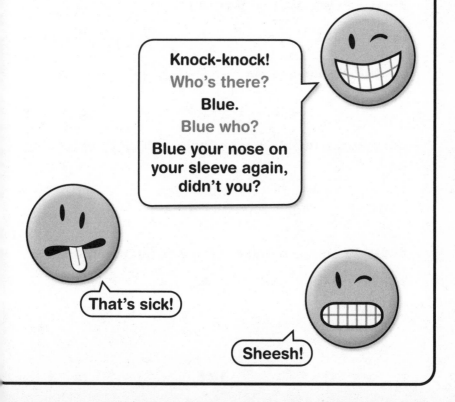

Knock-knock!
Who's there?
Blue.
Blue who?
Blue your nose on your sleeve again, didn't you?

That's sick!

Sheesh!

'SNOT FUNNY

When is a booger not a booger?

When it's snot.

Which nut catches the most colds?

The cashew.

What can you tie boogers into?

A snot.

Where does your nose go when it gets hungry?

Booger King.

What is the difference between a booger and a plate?

The plate goes ON the table. The booger goes UNDER the table.

What do boogers and apples have in common?

They both get picked and eaten.

What's the difference between boogers and brussels sprouts?

Kids won't eat brussels sprouts.

What did the booger say when the team captains were choosing players?

"Pick me! Pick me!"

What do you find in a clean nose?

Fingerprints!

What happens when you sneeze without using a tissue?

You take matters into your own hands.

Why do elephants have long fingernails?

So they can pick their trunks.

Who was hiding under little Sammy's bed?

The boogie man.

Which king plays a bagpipe, wears a kilt, and sneezes all the time?

The King of Snotland.

What did the booger say to his girlfriend?

"I'm stuck on you."

'SNOT FUNNY

What's green and hangs from a tree?

Giraffe snot.

Why do farmers have noses?

So they have something to pick while they wait for their crops to grow.

Why didn't the nose make the volleyball team?

Nobody picked him.

Why shouldn't you eat boogers?

Because you don't want to spoil your dinner.

Why is a haunted handkerchief scary?

Because it's covered in boo-gers.

Why don't dinosaurs pick their noses?

Because they don't want to eat 20-pound boogers.

Why was the snowman looking for carrots at the grocery store?

He wanted to pick his nose.

What runs in big families?

The same thing that runs in small families: noses.

How do you make a tissue dance?
Put a little boogy in it!

What did one booger say to the other?
"You think you're funny but you're snot."

What's gross?
Finding a hair in your food.
What's grosser than gross?
Finding out it's your grandma's nose hair.

Why do gorillas have large nostrils?
Because they have fat fingers.

When is a fence like a nose?
When it's a picket fence.

What did the big booger say to the little booger?
"Don't get snotty with me!"

What do you call a booger that's wearing a helmet?
A snail.

What do you do if your nose goes on strike?
Picket.

'SNOT FUNNY

Why did the booger cross the road?

Because he was being picked on.

Why do farmers have noses?

So they'll have something to pick in the winter.

What happened when the elephant sat on a quarter?

A booger popped out of George Washington's nose.

What's yellow and gooey and smells like bananas?

Monkey snot.

Why was the nose sad?

It didn't get picked.

What's in a ghost's nose?

Boo-gers.

Knock-knock!
Who's there?
Adam's not.
Adam's not who?
**Adam's not is dripping
from his nose.**

Knock-knock!
Who's there?
Decode.
Decode who?
**Decode in my nose
is getting worse.**

WHO FARTED?

Did you hear the joke about the fart?
It stinks.

What's the smelliest UFO?
An Unidentified Farting Object.

Sam and Janet are taking a walk when Sam lets out a huge fart.
"Ugh," says Janet, "please stop it!"
"I would," replies Sam, "but I don't know which way it went."

How do you tell one end of a worm from the other?
Put it in a bowl of flour and wait for it to fart.

Who wears a red cape and farts in the forest?
Little Rude Riding Hood.

How does a ghost fart?
Out of its boo-ty.

WHO FARTED?

What do you get if you fart on your birthday?

A birthday farty.

What happened when the kid held his breath to stop himself from burping?

He farted.

Why did the taxi driver fart?

Because his cab ran out of gas.

How is a ninja like a fart?

They're both silent but deadly.

Which Egyptian ruler farted a lot?

King Tootincoming.

What's invisible and smells like carrots?

Bunny farts!

What did the skunk say when the wind changed directions?

"It's all coming back to me now!"

How are rainbows made?

When unicorns fart.

Why should you only put 239 beans in bean soup?

One more would make it too farty (240).

Why did the skeleton burp?

Because it didn't have the guts to fart.

What do you call a king's fart?

Noble gas.

What place should you avoid if you don't want to fart?

The gas station.

What's the one thing a person won't do after they fart?

Admit it.

When does a boy take a bubble bath?

When he eats beans for dinner.

Why can't you smell alien farts?

Because they're out of this world.

What do you call a cat who likes to eat beans?

Puss 'n Toots.

WHO FARTED?

Two flies sit on a pile of poop. One fly passes gas. The other fly looks at him and says, "Hey, do you mind? I'm eating here."

What do you call someone who doesn't fart in public?

A private tooter.

What do you get when you mix a matchstick and a fart?

A flamethrower.

What hits the nose when aimed at the feet?

A fart.

Why don't bees fart?

Their stingers might fall off.

Knock-knock!
Who's there?
Gas.
Gas who?
Gas who just farted!

What is the sharpest thing in the world?

A fart. It goes through your pants and doesn't even leave a hole.

How are snowflakes made?

When snowmen fart.

What do you call a professional farter?

A tutor.

What causes cold winter winds?

Frosty the Snowman eating beans.

What did the mouse say when he found his favorite cheese in cubes?

Who cut the cheese?

Did you hear about the man who went to jail for air pollution?

His farts were just that bad.

How can you tell when a moth farts?

He flies straight for a second.

What happens when a clown farts?

It smells funny.

What happened when the kid ate baked beans before church?

He had to sit in his own pew.

WHO FARTED?

What do you get when you mix beans and onions?
Tear gas.

How is a filling station like a burrito?
They both supply you with gas.

What did the underwear say to the fart?
It's time for a change.

Why should you never fart in an Apple store?
Because they don't have Windows.

Why did little Johnny Gass win the race?
Because nobody wanted to pass Gass.

How do you know when Grandpa's getting old?
When he farts, dust comes out.

Why did the fart get in trouble at the library?
Because he was too loud.

Where did Cinderella go to the bathroom?
In a land fart, fart away.

What's invisible and smells like bananas?
A monkey fart.

BR-A-A-AINS!

Why did the zombie eat the archer?
He wanted his bone and marrow.

Why did the zombie go to the dentist?
To improve his bite.

What is the zombie's favorite TV show?
Chomping on the Stars.

Why did the little zombie stay home from school?
He was feeling rotten.

Why didn't the zombie cross the freeway?
Because he didn't have the guts.

Where do zombies live?
On dead-end streets.

Zombie Kid: Mom, Why do you look so tired?
Mombie: Because I'm dead on my feet.

BR-A-A-AINS!

Why did the zombie cross the road?
To eat the chicken.

What's a zombie's favorite meal?
A Manwich.

What's black and white and dead all over?
A zombie in a tuxedo.

What kind of engagement ring did the zombie give his girlfriend?
A tombstone.

What did the zombie say when he saw his favorite movie star?
"I've been dying to eat you!"

When do zombies wake up?
At ate-o'clock.

Why did the zombie take a nap?
He was dead tired.

Why do zombies only date smart girls?
They just love a woman with br-a-a-ains.

THE GROSSEST JOKES EVER!

When zombies break into a house, where do they look for food?

In the living room.

What did the zombie say to the other zombie who wanted to fight?

"You wanna piece of me?"

What kind of birds do zombies like to eat the most?

Cra-a-anes!

Why did the zombie sprinkle cheese powder on people's feet?

He wanted Doritoes.

Did you hear about the zombie hairdresser?

She dyed on the job.

Do dark circles around the eyes make a zombie look dead?

No, but being dead does.

What should you do if zombies surround your house?

Pray that it's Halloween.

What was the zombie kid's favorite game?

Corpse and robbers.

BR-A-A-AINS!

Why did the zombie eat the gym teacher?
He liked health food.

Why didn't the zombie finish eating the clown?
He tasted funny.

What did the zombie eat after its teeth were pulled?
The dentist.

What does a vegetarian zombie like to eat?
Gra-a-ains!

What did the zombie say to the locksmith?
"You're out of lock."

Which candy do zombie kids refuse?
Life Savers.

Why did the zombie eat a bowl of Cheerios?
He wanted to be a cereal killer.

Why did the zombie ignore his new Facebook friends?
He was busy digesting his old Facebook friends.

What do zombies like to eat at Christmastime?
Candy ca-a-anes!

What does a zombie order at a restaurant?
The waiter.

What did the zombie say to the watchmaker?
"Your time is up."

Zombie Kid: Mommy, do I have Daddy's eyes?
Mombie: Yes, dear. Now eat them before they get too cold.

What do you get when you cross a zombie with a snowman?
Frostbite.

How can you tell if a zombie is upset?
It falls to pieces.

What kind of bread do healthy zombies eat?
100 percent whole brain.

What's the zombie's favorite type of weather?
When it ra-a-a-ains!

How did the zombie ace the math test?
It was a no-brainer.

What does a zombie like to put on his br-a-a-ains?

Grave-y.

What's grosser than a dead zombie in the trash can?

A dead zombie in three thrash cans.

Why did the rotting zombie quit teaching?

She only had one pupil.

What do you call an undead wasp?

A zom-bee.

Do zombies eat popcorn with their fingers?

No, they eat the fingers separately.

Why did the zombie go crazy?

He had lost his mind.

Why are skeletons such great learners?

They can't help but to keep an open mind.

What do you call a vegetarian with diarrhea?
A salad shooter.

Why did the superhero flush the toilet?
It was his duty.

Why can't you hear a pterodactyl going to the bathroom?
Because the "p" is silent.

What is brown and sticky?
A stick.

Who is the most constipated of all artists?
Vincent Can't Go.

Toothbrush: I hate my job.
Toilet paper: You think your job stinks? Try mine!

Why is pea soup more special than mashed potatoes?
Because anyone can mash potatoes.

What did the rooster say when he stepped in a cow pie?

"Cock-a-doodle-poo!"

What isn't an elephant a good pet?

It takes too long to clean the litter box.

Who lives in the toilet and fights crime with ninja powers?

The Teenage Mutant Ninja Turdles.

What vegetables belong in a toilet?

Peas.

What's brown and sounds like a bell?

DUNGGGGGG!

Mother: Billy! Why are you sitting on the toilet and hitting yourself on the head?

Billy: Works for ketchup!

What do you call a part-time teacher who eats beans for lunch?

A substi-toot.

Why was the sand wet?

Because the sea weed.

What is big, green, and incredibly smelly?

The Hulk's farts!

Why did Captain Kirk go into the ladies' room?

He wanted to go where no man had gone before.

Your feet are so smelly, your shoes hide in the closet and refuse to come out.

Why couldn't the toilet paper cross the road?

It got stuck in a crack.

Student: May I go to the bathroom?

Teacher: Yes, but say your ABCs first.

Student: A B C D E F G H I J K L M N O Q R S T U V W X Y Z.

Teacher: Where is the P?

Student: Running down my leg.

Whaddaya call it when you go #1 before watching a movie?

A pee-quel.

Doctor: Four out of five people suffer from diarrhea.

Patient: Does that mean that one person enjoys it?

What's dumb?

Directions on toilet paper.

What's dumber than that?

Reading them.

Even dumber than that?

Reading them and learning something.

The dumbest of all?

Reading them and having to correct something that you've been doing wrong.

If you're an American outside the bathroom, what are you inside the bathroom?

European!

What happens when babies eat Rice Krispies?

Snap, crackle, poop!

Did you hear the one about the elephant with diarrhea?

You should have, it's all over town.

What do you get if you cross a worm and a goat?

A dirty kid.

If there's H_2O on the inside of a fire hydrant, what's on the outside?

K9P.

How do website developers ask each other where the bathroom is?

"Can you tell me the IP address?"

Why didn't anyone see the movie about constipation?

It never came out.

What do you get when you cross a dinosaur with a skunk?

A U-stink-asaurus.

What do flies and stinky feet have in common?

You can shoe them, but they never go away.

Why did the man bring a toilet to the party?

He was a party pooper.

Your toenails are so long, you can cut the grass by walking barefoot.

What did the judge say when the skunk walked into the courtroom?

"Odor in the court!"

Thieves broke into the police station and stole all of the toilets. The police are investigating, but for now...they have nothing to go on.

What is the stinkiest dog?

The poo-dle.

Where did the rainbow go to the bathroom?

In the pot of gold.

Why did Tigger stick his head in the toilet?

He was looking for Pooh.

What do you call it when you step in alien droppings?

A close encounter of the turd kind.

Flatulence: The emergency vehicle that picks you up after you are run over by a steamroller.

Why did the roll of toilet paper quit its job?

It was pooped.

Farting on an elevator is wrong on so many levels.

What did the first mate see when he looked down the toilet?

The captain's log.

What do they say about a bird in the hand?

It can't poop on your head.

How do you keep flies out of the kitchen?

Put a big pile of manure in the living room.

Why did the fart cross the road?

It was trying to escape the stink.

Fart: A turd honking for the right of way.

Did you hear about Robin Hood's toilet?

He had a Little John.

What has two legs, one wheel, and stinks?

A wheelbarrow full of manure.

What's a volcano?

A mountain with the runs.

Where do bees go to the bathroom?

The BP station.

Did you hear the joke about the trash truck?

Never mind, it's garbage.

Knock-knock!
Who's there?
Butternut.
Butternut who?
Butternut step
in the steaming pile
of horse manure!

Knock-knock!
Who's there?
Enid.
Enid who?
Enid a clean
pair of
underwear NOW!

Knock-knock!
Who's there?
European.
European who?
European all
over the floor!

Knock-knock!
Who's there?
Snow.
Snow who?
Snow fun
to clean up
elephant poop.

Knock-knock!
Who's there?
Distinct.
Distinct who?
Distinct of
skunk is awful!

Knock-knock!
Who's there?
Sabrina.
Sabrina who?
Sabrina long time
since I changed
my underwear!

DON'T EAT THAT!

Why couldn't the snake talk?
He had a frog in his throat.

What do cats eat for breakfast?
Mice Krispies.

What's green, fuzzy, and sits in a bun?
A school lunch hamburger.

What's green, fuzzy, and sits on a toilet for hours?
The kid who ate the school lunch hamburger.

What's the difference between a worm and a blueberry?
Have you ever tried eating a worm pie?

How do you keep a loaf of bread warm all day?
Let a cat sleep on it.

What did the spider order at McDonald's?
French flies.

DON'T EAT THAT!

What do you call a worm in an apple?

Teacher's pet.

How do you make a maggot stew?

Keep the maggot waiting for a couple of hours.

What's the difference between school lunch and a pair of smelly socks?

In an emergency, you can eat the smelly socks.

Which cafeteria food makes you throw up?

Spew-ghetti.

Kid: Mommy! Mommy! What happened to the dry dog food Fido wouldn't eat?

Mom: Be quiet and eat your cereal.

What do you get when you cross a turkey with a centipede?

Drumsticks for everybody!

Why did the farmer eat his foot?

Because there was a corn on it.

What's a mushroom?

The place they store school lunches.

What's sticky, purple, has 16 legs, and is covered with thick, brown hair?

I don't know, but it's on your lunch tray.

How do you know that owls are smarter than chickens?

Have you ever eaten fried owl?

What do you get when you throw up Chef Boyardee canned pasta?

Barf-a-Roni.

Why didn't Batman go fishing?

Because Robin ate all the worms.

What's green, comes on a bun, and is covered in ketchup and mustard?

A hot frog.

What did the royal taster say after he drank the poisoned water?

Not much.

What's the difference between school lunch and a pile of manure?

School lunches are usually served cold.

Patient: Doctor, doctor, I've had a horrible stomachache since I ate a plate of oysters yesterday.

Doctor: Were they fresh?

Patient: I have no idea.

Doctor: How did they look when you opened the shells?

Patient: I was supposed to open the shells?

How do you make a slug drink?

Stick it in the blender.

A science teacher is teaching class. "In this bag, I have a frog, and we're going to dissect it," she says. She turns the bag over and a turkey sandwich rolls out. "That's odd," she says. "I distinctly remember eating my lunch."

Whaddaya call an unsolicited e-mail that advertises processed meat?

Spam spam.

What's green and has holes in it?

Moldy Swiss cheese.

How do you do an impression of a bird?

Eat a worm.

Why do lions eat raw meat?

Because they don't know how to cook.

Foods not eaten on the *Titanic*: Life Savers and root beer floats.

When is a slug a vegetable?

After you squash it.

What do pigs eat on hot days?

Slopsicles.

What's the worst thing in the school cafeteria?

The food.

Why was the sword swallower arrested?

He coughed and killed two people.

What's grosser than finding a worm in your apple?

Finding half a worm.

What did the Komodo dragon say when it saw a flock of turkeys?

"Gobble! Gobble!"

DON'T EAT THAT!

What's the difference between a slug and a peanut butter sandwich?

Slugs don't stick to the roof of your mouth.

What tastes worse than grape jam?

Toe jam.

Why do vultures prefer bad restaurants?

The food is rotten.

What's the difference between a grasshopper and an éclair?

A grasshopper has more cream filling.

What is the difference between school lunch and a pile of slugs?

School lunch comes on a plate.

Did you hear about the dog who ate garlic?

His bark was worse than his bite.

What do ants like on their pizza?

Antchovies.

What's gray and furry on the inside and white on the outside?

A mouse sandwich.

What happens to a daddy longlegs when it hides in a salad?

It becomes a daddy shortlegs.

What's the difference between head lice and dandruff?

Head lice are crunchier.

What happens if you eat yeast and shoe polish before bed?

You'll rise and shine in the morning.

What's the difference between a worm and a cookie?

A worm doesn't fall apart when you dunk it in milk.

Why did the boy eat the firefly?

He wanted a light snack.

What's the hardest vegetable to swallow?

The artichoke.

How do lunch ladies keep flies out of the cafeteria?

They let them taste the food.

DON'T EAT THAT!

Why should you finish your plate when you eat school lunch?

So it won't be someone else's lunch tomorrow.

How are roaches like raisins?

They both show up in oatmeal.

Mommy! Mommy! What happened to all your scabs?

Be quiet and finish your corn flakes.

Why did the dog go to school at lunchtime?

He was part of the flea lunch program.

Why did the witch send her pizza back?

They forgot the cockroaches again.

Why don't dinosaurs eat at Burger King?

They have it their way wherever they eat!

What happens if you cross a cheeseburger with a yo-yo?

After you eat it, it comes back up again.

What do you get if you swallow plutonium?

Atomic ache.

Why did dinosaurs eat other dinosaurs?

Because it takes one to gnaw one.

What do you get if you cross barf with pasta?

Ralph-i-oli.

What's the best thing they've ever had in the school cafeteria?

A fire drill.

Can you define bacteria?

It's the rear entrance to the school cafeteria.

What happened when they threw out the school cafeteria leftovers?

The alley cats threw them back.

What do you get if you eat prune pizza?

Pizzeria.

How can you tell a mouse from spaghetti?

A mouse won't slip off your fork.

Why are frogs always so happy?

Because they eat whatever bugs them.

How do you make a cockroach float?

Throw it in a root beer and add two scoops of ice cream.

Why are false teeth like the stars?

Because they come out at night.

Why did the lunch lady put her thumb on the student's hamburger?

She didn't want it to fall on the floor again.

Monster mommy: Don't eat that uranium.

Little monster: Why not?

Mommy: You'll get atomic-ache.

What's the difference between a carrot and a unicorn?

The first is a bunny feast, the second is a funny beast.

CREATURE FEATURE

What kind of fish don't swim?
Dead ones.

How much money does a skunk have?
One scent.

Why was the man fired from the zoo for feeding the penguins?
Because he fed them to the lions.

What lies on the ground 100 feet up in the air?
A dead centipede.

What's grosser than a three-headed spider with 40 eyes?
Not much.

A three-legged dog walks into an Old West saloon. He sidles up to the bar and says, "I'm looking for the man who shot my paw."

CREATURE FEATURE

Where does a bee sit?

On its bee-hind.

What do you do if you find a boa constrictor in your toilet?

Wait until it's finished.

What do you get if you cross a Rottweiler and a St. Bernard?

A dog that bites off your arm and then goes for help.

What do you call a smelly sheep?

Ewwwwwe.

What goes *snap, crackle, pop*?

A dying firefly.

What do you call fishing if you don't catch any fish?

Drowning worms.

Why couldn't the vulture fly with two dead raccoons?

The plane only allowed one carrion per passenger.

What has five legs?

A lion carrying leftovers.

What's black and white and flat?

A penguin flattened by a steamroller.

What do you get when you cross a pig with a centipede?

Bacon and legs.

What do you get when you cross a T. rex with a dog?

Something that drinks out of any toilet it wants to.

**Birdy, birdy in the sky,
Dropped some white stuff in my eye.
I'm too big to whine or cry,
I'm just glad that cows don't fly!**

What has 50 legs but can't walk?

Half a centipede.

What do you get if you cross a bird with a cat?

A cat that isn't hungry anymore.

What's the last thing to go through a bug's mind when it hits the windshield?

Its backside.

CREATURE FEATURE

Two lions played poker for a giraffe. Why were they nervous?

The game was for high steaks.

Did you hear about the fly who put himself on the map?

He got squashed in an atlas.

What do you get when you cross a pig with a comedian?

Slopstick humor.

What goes "Eek-eek! Bang!"?

A mouse riding a firework.

Why didn't the veterinarian want to treat the toad?

She was afraid it would croak.

Why did the hen wash the chick's mouth out with soap?

He was using fowl language.

What's black and white and red all over?

An exploding zebra.

What do you call a bug that has worked its way to the top?

Head lice.

What's small, gray, sucks blood, and eats cheese?
A mouse-quito.

What does a Triceratops sit on?
Its Tricerabottom.

What's black and white and red all over?
A skunk with diaper rash.

Which reptile lives in the Emerald City?
The Lizard of Oz.

How do you stop an octopus from punching you?
Disarm it.

What's yellow, wiggly, and dangerous?
A maggot with a bad attitude.

What does a boa constrictor call its dinner date?
Dessert.

Why did the girl toss a snail out the window?
She wanted to see slime fly.

Little Skunk: Can I have a chemistry set for my birthday?
Skunk Mom: No way! You'll stink up the house!

Why did the chicken take a bath?

It smelled fowl.

What happened to the man who tried to cross a lion with a goat?

He had to get a new goat.

What do you say when you meet a toad?

Warts new?

What's black and white and green all over?

A seasick zebra.

What do you call a toothless bear?

A gummy bear.

What does a chicken say when it lays a square egg?

Ouch.

What do you call a frog with no back legs?

Unhoppy.

Why did John bring his skunk to school?

For show and smell.

YES WE CANNIBAL

Why do cannibals like weddings?
They get to toast the bride and groom.

What do cannibals call skateboarders?
Meals on wheels.

Did you hear about the cannibal lion with the big ego?
He had to swallow his pride.

Cannibal Kid: Dad, why can't I play with other kids?
Cannibal Dad: It's not polite to play with your food.

Why should you never upset a cannibal?
You'll end up in hot water.

How did the cannibal like his guests?
Medium well.

Cannibal Kid: Dad, I hate my math teacher.
Cannibal Dad: Then just eat your salad.

Why was the cannibal expelled from school?

She was caught buttering up the teacher.

Two explorers are walking through the forest when they get into an argument and start hitting each other. A cannibal who is spying on them yells, "Food fight!"

What's yellow and smells like people?

Cannibal barf.

Did you hear about the cannibal who thought he was a termite?

He only ate wooden legs.

What do cannibals call a bus filled with tourists?

A buffet.

Did you hear about the cannibal restaurant?

Dinner costs an arm and a leg.

Junior Cannibal: Mom! I brought a friend home for dinner.

Mommy Cannibal: Dinner is already on the table. Put your friend in the fridge and we'll have him tomorrow.

Did you hear about the cannibal who arrived late to the dinner party?

They gave him the cold shoulder.

Why did the cannibal eat the tightrope walker?

He wanted to eat a balanced diet.

What did the cannibal say to the waiter?

I'll have a large Manwich and a tossed Sally on the side.

What's a cannibal's favorite vegetable?

Human beans.

Why did the cannibal have twins in his lunch box?

Just in case he wanted seconds.

Why do cannibals make good police detectives?

Because they can really grill a suspect.

What does a cannibal eat when he's late for lunch?

Spare ribs.

What do cannibals call track stars?

Fast food.

What color is a hiccup?

Burple.

What goes "Ha-ha-ha-plop!"?

Someone laughing their head off.

Doctor, doctor, what's the best way to avoid biting insects?

Quit biting them.

There once was a lawman named Earp,
Who threw up all over some twerp.
At the OK Corral,
He said, "Sorry, pal!
I thought it was only a burp."

Why did the fisherman go to the doctor?

He lost his herring.

What happened when the butcher backed into the meat grinder?

He got a little behind in his work.

Why did the pig go to the eye doctor?

He had pink eye.

What do you call a person who sticks their right hand in an alligator's mouth?

Lefty.

What should you do if someone rolls their eyes at you?

Pick them up and roll them right back.

What has four legs and flies?

A dead cow.

What's green and curly?

A seasick poodle.

Mom: I thought I told you to drink your medicine after your bath.

Son: Sorry, Mom. After I finished drinking the bath, I couldn't drink another drop.

What's the difference between a peach and a wound?

One bruises easily, one oozes easily.

Nurse: The new doctor is really amusing. He'll leave you in stitches.

Patient: I hope not. I only came to collect my prescription.

What's yellow, lumpy, and flies through space?

Halley's Vomit.

Patient: Doctor, doctor! My stomach hurts. I've eaten three blue billiard balls, two red billiard balls, and an orange billiard ball.

Doctor: No wonder you aren't feeling well. You aren't getting enough greens.

What was the most common illness in the Jurassic period?

Dino-sore throats!

An apple a day keeps the doctor away. An onion a day keeps everyone away!

What did the teacher say when his glass eye went down the drain?

"Oh no, I've lost another pupil."

What's the difference between a dentist and a Yankees fan?

One roots for the Yanks and the other yanks for the roots.

Doctor: What's wrong with your wife?

Husband: She thinks she's a chicken.

Doctor: How long has she been this way?

Husband: For three years.

Doctor: Why didn't you call me sooner?

Husband: We needed the eggs.

What's the cure for dandruff?

Baldness.

Why did the lion throw up after eating Abraham Lincoln?

Because it's hard to keep a good man down.

Kid: Gramps? What's more important? Your money or your health?

Gramps: Your health, kiddo. Without your health, you're a goner.

Kid: Great. So can you lend me $20?

Fight air pollution. Gargle with mouthwash!

What do you get when you combine a drawing toy with vomit?

A Retch-a-Sketch.

Dentist: You've got the biggest cavity I've ever seen. You've got the biggest cavity I've ever seen.

Patient: You didn't have to say it twice.

Dentist: I didn't. That was an echo.

Why did the old man cover his mouth when he sneezed?

So his teeth wouldn't fly out.

Why don't zombies eat weathermen?

They give them wind.

Where does a one-handed man shop?

In a second-hand store.

What animal always pukes after it eats?

A yak.

A man and a woman went on the road with their animal impressions act. She did the sounds, and he did...the smells.

Where's the best place to save toenail clippings?

In a nail file.

Painful Reading: *Epic Fails!* by S. Platt

THE GROSSEST JOKES EVER!

What should you give a seasick hippo?
Space.

Doctor, doctor, what's good for biting fingernails?
Very sharp teeth.

Why were the barber's hands so dirty?
No one had been in for a shampoo all day.

What do you call a sick alligator?
An ill-igator.

How did the dentist become a brain surgeon?
His hand slipped.

What happened when the boy drank 8 colas?
He burped 7-up.

How do you catch dandruff?
Shake your head over a paper bag.

Doctor, doctor! How can I stop my nose from running?
Stick your foot out and trip it.

What was Beethoven doing in his grave?
Decomposing.

THAT'S SICK

What's green, sticky, and smells like eucalyptus?
Koala vomit.

What's wet, stinks, and goes *thump thump thump*?
A skunk in the dryer.

What does a sick dog say?
Barf! Barf! Barf!

How do you get kids to stop biting their toenails?
Make them wear shoes.

Doctor, doctor! What should I do about my yellow teeth?
Wear a brown tie.

What do you call the first person to discover fire?
Crispy.

What's it called when you throw up on an airplane?
Jet gag.

Did you hear the one about the foot?
It's pretty corny.

Did you hear the one about the fungus?
It grows on you.

ed effort

THE GROSSEST JOKES EVER!

What's yellow, lumpy, and smells like a zebra?
Lion puke.

Patient: Doc! Why can't I feel my legs?
Doctor: Because I had to amputate your hands.

Why did the mummy go to the doctor?
He was as pale as a ghost.

Who throws up more than any other little boy in the world?
Retchy Retch.

Doctor! Doctor! I swallowed a spoon!
Try to relax, and don't stir.

What's small, cuddly, and bright purple?
A koala holding its breath.

What's the best airline to get sick on?
Spew-nited Airlines.

Why did T. rex need a bandage?
Because he had a dino-sore.

Patient: Doctor, my feet keep falling asleep.
Doctor: Try wearing loud socks.

Why did the toad cross the road?

To show everybody that he had guts.

What is a rat's favorite game?

Hide and squeak.

Why do rats avoid water?

Catfish.

What do you call a fairy that pees a lot?

Tinklebell.

Which Scottish creature eats raw salmon at every meal?

The Lox Ness Monster.

Why did the space shuttle pilot eat beans every day?

He didn't want to run out of gas.

MONSTER MASH

Why does the mummy walk funny?
Monster wedgie.

What is Dracula's favorite fruit?
Necktarines.

Why was the blob turned away from the restaurant?
No shirt, no shoes, no service.

Why was Dracula thrown out of the butcher shop?
He was caught chop-lifting.

Why did Death carry a broom instead of a scythe?
He wanted to be the Grim Sweeper.

What do sea monsters eat?
Fish and ships.

Why wouldn't the other little monsters play with Dracula's children?
They were vampire brats.

What do you get when you cross a vampire and a gnome?

A creature that sucks blood from your kneecaps.

Junior: Mom! Everyone at school says I look like a werewolf! Am I?

Mom: Don't be silly. Now go comb your face.

Why do vampires drink blood?

Root beer makes them burp.

What does Godzilla like to spread on his toast?

Traffic jams.

Why was Frankenstein's monster furious at his creator?

Because Dr. Frankenstein overcharged him.

I have a green nose, three red mouths, and four purple ears. What am I?

Monstrous!

Why did the vampire call the morgue?

To see if they delivered.

Little Monster: Mommy! Mommy! When is the pool going to be ready?

Momster: I don't know, but just keep spitting.

Why don't girls like Dracula?

He has bat breath.

How does a monster count to 13?

On his fingers.

What do you do with a green monster?

Put it in the sun until it ripens.

Boy Monster: Did you get the big red heart I sent you for Valentine's Day?

Girl Monster: Yes, I did. But it stopped beating. Can you send me another one?

Why do skeletons play the piano?

They don't have organs.

What do you call a 50-pound hornet with a slime gun?

Sir.

Why did the dragon burn down his own house?

He liked home cooking.

Why doesn't Death ever miss a phone call?

He has a grim beeper.

Why wouldn't the vampire eat his soup?

It had clotted.

What do you get if you cross a long-fanged, purple-spotted monster with a cat?

A town with no dogs.

Why didn't Count Dracula ever shower?

He was filthy rich.

Which monster makes the worst houseguest?

The Loch Mess Monster.

Nurse: What is your blood type?

Vampire: I'm not picky. Any type will do.

What's a vampire's favorite ice cream?

Veinilla.

What do little ghosts wear in the rain?

Ghoulashes!

Why did Frankenstein go to see a psychiatrist?

He had a screw loose.

How did the vampire hunters find Count Dracula's hidden lair?

He was coffin in his sleep.

What type of dogs do vampires like best?

Bloodhounds.

Why did the Kraken eat the pirate ship?

He wanted Cap'n Crunch for breakfast.

Which vampire liked to fly kites in thunderstorms?

Benjamin Fanglin.

Where did the skeleton keep his pet canary?

In a rib cage.

Which circus performers do vampires like best?

The jugulars.

What's a sea monster's favorite sandwich?

A sub.

What do you call a deer with no eyes?
No eye-deer.

What do you call a deer with no eyes and no legs?
Still no eye-deer!

Did you hear about the magician who likes to include his siblings in his act?
Now he has two half-sisters and one half-brother.

What's the most violent job?
Chef—because they beat eggs and whip cream.

What kind of ball should you never play with?
An eyeball.

Where are dead potatoes buried?
In gravy-yards.

Why is it so hard to get a job as a sword fighter?
The competition is cutthroat.

What do you call a dog with no legs?

It doesn't matter. He won't come anyway.

What do you DO with a dog with no legs?

Take him for a drag!

What do you get when you cross an alligator and a parrot?

I don't know, but if it asks for a cracker, better give it the whole box!

Why did Mickey Mouse get hit in the head with a rock?

Because Donald ducked.

Did you hear about the stupid coyote?

He got stuck in a trap, chewed off three of his legs...and was still stuck.

What did the dumb bunny do when his computer froze?

He put it in the microwave.

Patient: Doc, you gotta help me! I broke my arm in two places!

Doctor: Try avoiding those places in the future.

LAST GASP

How do you make a dumb bunny laugh on Tuesday?

Tell him a joke on Sunday.

Why did little Sammy feed birdseed to his cat?

Because that's where his canary was.

Patient: Doc, you gotta help me! When I drink hot chocolate, I get a stabbing pain in my right eye.

Doctor: Try taking the spoon out of the cup.

Favorite Western Movie: *Gunslingers with Gas* starring Wyatt Urp

What do you call a cow that just gave birth?

Decalfinated.

Why is it dangerous to do math in the jungle?

Because if you add 4 and 4, you get ate.

Did you hear about the cow that tried to jump over a barbed-wire fence?

It was an udder disaster.

Why did half a chicken cross the road?

To get to its other side.

**Patient: Doc, you gotta help me!
I've become invisible!**

Doctor: Sorry, I can't see you now.

**What did the half-man/half-bull say before
going to the store?**

"I'll be back in a minotaur."

**Two goldfish are sitting in a tank. One says to
the other: "You drive, I'll man the guns."**

What stands in the field and says "mmmmm"?

A cow with its lips glued together.

What do you call a man with a shovel in his head?

Doug.

Why do elephants stomp on people?

They like the squishy feeling between their toes.

What do you get if you cross a bird with a fan?

Shredded tweet.

**Favorite Bathroom Reading: *Fifty Yards to the
Outhouse* by Willy Makit; Foreword by Betty Wont**

What's brown and sits on a piano bench?

Beethoven's last movement.

Jo: Our new dog is like a member of the family.
Flo: I can see the resemblance!

What was the Blob's favorite drink?
Slime-ade!

When does a car really stink?
When it's full of gas.

How a pimple keeps its shape: Zitups!

Why did the skunk cross the road?
To get to the odor side.

Suzie: Dad, are worms good to eat?
Dad: Why do you ask?
Suzie: Because there was one in your salad.

What happened when the thief fell into wet cement?
He became a hardened criminal.

Why did the toilet paper roll down the mountain?
To get to the bottom.

Knock-knock!
Who's there?
One shoe.
One shoe who?
**One shoe bathe
every once in awhile?**

What happened when the cat ate Mexican jumping beans?

Its poop jumped out of the litter box.

What do you get when you cross a whale with a sea slug?

Moby ick!

Red Riding Hood's Favorite Book: *Chased by a Wolf* by Claude Bottom

Dog Owner: I think my dog has ticks. What should I do?

Veterinarian: Stop winding him.

How did the astronaut suffocate?

He farted in his space suit.

Book you'll never see: *Yellow River* by I.P. Freely

What gave Godzilla a bellyache?

Someone he ate.

What shoots stuffing across the room?

A farting turkey.

What kind of monster can sit on the end of your finger?

The boogeyman.

Why do noses run?

Because they can't walk.

Why didn't the viper viper nose?

Because the adder adder handkerchief.

Student: Do you have holes in your underwear?

Teacher: Of course not!

Student: Then how did you get your feet through them?

How do bugs say "Merry Christmas"?

"Fleas Navidad!"

How are little brothers like laxatives?

They irritate the poop out of you.

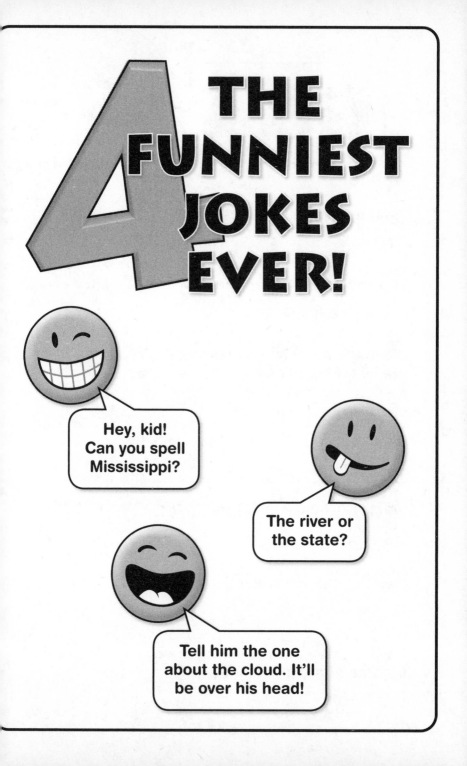

What do you call a kid captured by a cannibal?
Stu!

What do you get when you cross a bear with a skunk?
Winnie the Pew.

When the moth hit the windshield, what was the last thing to go through its mind?
Its butt!

What do you call a cow with a twitch?
Beef jerky.

What do you call a hippy's wife?
Mississippi.

How does Darth Vader like his toast?
On the dark side!

If we breathe oxygen during the day, what do we breathe at night?
Nightrogen.

What's the hardest thing about learning to skate?
The ground!

What kind of bagel can fly?
A plain bagel.

Why shouldn't you write with a broken pencil?
It's pointless.

Why couldn't the gnome pay his rent?
He was a little short.

What do you call a prehistoric pig?
Jurassic pork!

Why is it dangerous to do math in the jungle?
Because if you add 4 and 4, you get ate.

Why did dinosaurs walk so slowly?
Because running shoes hadn't been invented yet.

Why did the little strawberry cry?
Her mom and dad were in a jam.

Why did the rooster cross the road?
It was the chicken's day off.

Q&A

What do you call a fake noodle?
An impasta.

Why don't zombies eat clowns?
They taste funny!

What do you give to a sick lemon?
Lemon aid.

Who makes the best exploding underwear?
Fruit of the Boom!

What do you call a grizzly bear caught in a rain shower?
A drizzly bear.

What kind of songs are balloons afraid of?
Pop songs!

What is every magician's favorite candy bar?
Twix.

What's white, furry, and shaped like a tooth?
A molar bear.

Did you hear about the computer program created by a chicken?

All you do is point and cluck.

What did the alpaca say when she was kicked off the farm?

"Alpaca my bags!"

What's the most important rule for doing science experiments?

Never lick the spoon.

What would bears be without bees?

Ears!

What do you give a seasick monster?

Plenty of room!

Why did the cowboy ride the bull?

It was too heavy to carry.

Which Great Lake do ghosts like best?

Lake Eerie.

Why do the French eat snails?

Because they don't like fast food.

How did the frozen chicken cross the road?
In a shopping bag.

What do you call a rabbit with fleas?
Bugs Bunny.

If athletes get athlete's feet, what do astronauts get?
Missile toe!

Why can't you hear a pterodactyl going to the bathroom?
Because the "p" is silent.

What do you get when you crossa goat with a squid?
Billy the Squid.

Have you heard the joke about the peach?
It's pitiful.

Which bird can hold three gallons of water in its bill?
The pelican.

Where does Spider-Man go for medical advice?
Web MD.

THE FUNNIEST JOKES EVER!

Why was the potato alone at the party?
It got there oily.

What's the best time to visit the dentist?
Tooth-hurty!

Which state needs a handkerchief?
Mass-ACHOO!-setts.

Why do fish choirs always sing off-key?
Because you can't tuna fish.

What kind of undies do clouds wear?
Thunderwear!

Did you hear about the frog that was illegally parked?
It got toad.

Why did the toilet paperroll down the hill?
To get to the bottom.

If April showers bring May flowers, what do May flowers bring?
Pilgrims!

What do you call a motorcycle with a good sense of humor?
A Yamahahaha.

Q&A

Why did the kid leave his piggy bank outside?
He expected some change in the weather.

Why didn't the teddy bear eat his oatmeal?
He was already stuffed!

What kind of books do skunks read?
Best-smellers.

Why do vampires brush their teeth?
To prevent bat breath.

Where do baby ghosts spend their days?
At day-scare centers.

What do you call a sleeping T. rex?
A dino-snore!

Why did the cantaloupe jump into the lake?
It wanted to be a watermelon.

Why did the belt get arrested?
It held up a pair of pants.

Why are batteries always sad?
Because they're never included.

How can you fall off a 100-foot ladder without getting hurt?

Easy! Fall from the bottom rung.

How is Facebook like a refrigerator?

Because every few minutes you open it to see if there's anything good in it.

If Pilgrims were alive today, what would they be most famous for?

Their age!

What's the best day to go to the beach?

Sun-day.

What do baby sweet potatoes wear to bed?

Their yammies!

What's green, has big eyes, and is hard to see through?

Kermit the Fog.

What kind of car does a farmer drive?

A corn-vertible.

Where do you send a shoe in the summer?

Boot camp!

Why were the early days of history called the Dark Ages?

Because there were so many knights.

What did one car muffler say to the other car muffler?

"Boy, am I exhausted!"

What should you shout if you swim into kelp and get caught in it?

"Kelp!"

What lives at the bottom of the ocean and is popular on Easter?

Oyster eggs.

What do you say to a hitchhiking angel?

"Harp in!"

How do you make antifreeze?

Steal her blanket.

What has a big mouth but can't talk?

A jar.

What's red and smells like blue paint?

Red paint.

DOGS & CATS

Which kind of dog can jump higher than a building?
Any dog. Buildings can't jump.

What looks like half of a cat?
The other half.

What do cats like to eat for dessert?
Mice cream.

What should you know before you teach a dog a trick?
More than the dog!

Which movie is a feline favorite?
The Sound of Mew-sic.

Why can dogs scratch whenever they want to?
They live in a flea country.

What did the alien say to the cat?
"Take me to your litter!"

Will: If you want to find your dog,
you should put an ad in the paper.

Bill: Don't be silly. Fido can't read!

Which cats make the best bowlers?

Alley cats.

Why are dogs such terrible dancers?

They have two left feet.

How do you spell mousetrap using three letters?

C-A-T!

What did the dog say when it sat on the sandpaper?

Ruff.

Cat: What smells the most in a garbage dump?

Rat: The nose.

Which household cleaner do dalmatians fear most?

Spot remover.

What do you call a guy who's been attacked by a cat?

Claude!

Why did the dog say "Meow"?

He was trying to learn a second language.

What's a cat's favorite song?

"Three Blind Mice."

What do you get when you cross a dog and a dandelion?

A collie-flower.

Which game do cats like to play with mice?

Catch!

Where do dogs go when their tails fall off?

The retail store.

How do cats end a fight?

They hiss and make up.

What did the dalmatian say after eating?

"That hit the spots!"

What's smarter than a talking cat?

A spelling bee.

How do fleas get from one dog to another dog?

By itch-hiking.

Why was the kitten in such a bad mood?
She needed a catnap.

Why did the dog cross the road...twice?
To fetch a boomerang!

What do cats like to put in their milk?
Mice cubes.

Which breed of dog loves taking baths?
Shampoodles!

Why do cats scratch themselves?
Because no one else knows where the itch is.

How do you keep a dog from smelling?
Put a clothespin on its nose.

Why can't cats finish watching DVDs?
They can't resist pressing the "paws" button.

What did one flea say to the other flea when they walked out of the movie?
"Shall we walk or take the dog?"

What do you call a giant pile of cats?
A meowtain.

What do sheepdogs turn into every summer?
Hot dogs!

Why are cats terrible storytellers?
They only have one tail.

Why do dogs run around in circles?
It's hard to run around in squares.

What breakfast cereal do cats like best?
Mice Krispies!

Why did the Dachshund bite his trainer's ankle?
He couldn't reach any higher.

What do you call a cat that just swallowed a duck?
A duck-filled fatty puss.

When is a bloodhound dumb?
When it has no scents.

Why do cats climb trees?
Because they don't have ladders.

Why did the terrier have splinters in his tongue?
He kept eating table scraps.

When is it bad luck to have a black cat cross your path?

When you're a mouse!

Which holiday do dogs like best?

Howl-o-ween.

What do you get if you cross a rabbit with two cats?

Hare! Kitty kitty!

Which dogs make the best teachers?

Grade Danes.

How can you tell if a cat burglar has been in your house?

Your cat is missing.

Adopting and training a new puppy can be a real challenge at first. Yeah, it's ruff!

How do dog catchers get paid?

By the pound.

Dogs go to obedience school, but young cats go to class, too...Kittygarten!

What does Godzilla eat at a restaurant?
The restaurant!

Why couldn't the bagel escape?
It was covered with lox.

What kind of candy do you eat on the playground?
Recess Pieces.

Why did the beet turn red?
It saw the salad dressing.

Did you hear about the crazy pancake?
He just flipped!

What is Peter Pan's favorite fast-food restaurant?
Wendy's.

Who makes shoes for fruit?
A peach cobbler.

How do you fix a broken pizza?

With tomato paste.

Who writes nursery rhymes and squeezes oranges?

Mother Juice.

Kid: Waiter! There's a bee in my soup.

Waiter: Of course. You ordered alphabet soup.

What was the snowman's favorite cereal?

Frosted Flakes.

Which food can you eat in the bathroom?

Showerkraut.

What's green, has 22 legs, and plays football?

The Green Bay Pickles.

Why did the pie go to the dentist?

It needed a filling.

What's brown, wrinkled, and lives in a tower?

The Lunch Bag of Notre Dame.

What do you get when you cross a pig and a centipede?

Bacon and legs.

Why did the baker stop making doughnuts?
He was tired of the hole business.

Did you hear about the guy who drank food coloring?
He dyed a little inside.

What starts with a T, ends with a T, and is full of T?
A teapot.

What does the ocean eat for breakfast?
Boatmeal.

Why are tightrope walkers so healthy?
They always eat a balanced diet.

What do computers snack on?
Microchips.

What do you call a baby potato?
A small fry.

What did the baby corn say to the mama corn?
"Where's Popcorn?"

Why did the cookie visit the doctor?
It was feeling crummy.

YUM YUCKS!

What do you call a potato at a football game?

A spec-tater!

What was the anteater's favorite pizza topping?

Antchovies!

What do you get when you cross a bee with chopped meat?

Humburger.

What did the banana do when it saw a horde of hungry monkeys?

Split.

Why did the kid stare at the frozen orange juice can all day?

Because the label said "concentrate."

What does a nosy pepper do?

Gets jalapeño business.

A kid walks into a soda shop with a slab of asphalt under his arm and says, "A root beer please, and one for the road."

Which potato makes the best detective?

One whose eyes are peeled.

What did the hot dog say when it won the race?

"I'm a weiner!"

What happens when the chef goes on strike?

You have a cook-out.

What does a panda fry his bamboo in?

A pan...duh!

What did the frog order at McDonald's?

Flies and a diet croak.

Dad: Sorry, son, but I only know how to make two dishes, meat loaf and apple pie.

Son: Which one is this?

Why did the potato cross the road?

It saw a fork up ahead.

Best Cookbook: *Hot Dog* by Frank Furter

What did one plate say to the other plate?

"Lunch is on me!"

What kind of nut doesn't have a shell?

A doughnut.

YUM YUCKS!

Did you hear the joke about the pepperoni pizza?
Never mind. It's way too cheesy.

What kind of ice cream is bad at tennis?
Soft serve.

Which day do eggs hate?
Fry-day.

Which food stays hot in the fridge?
Hot dogs.

What do ghosts eat for lunch?
Boo-loney sandwiches.

What do you call a stolen yam?
A hot potato.

What do you call a small hot dog?
A teenie weenie!

How do you make soup into gold?
Add 14 carrots.

What does a snowman put in his coffee?
Cold cream.

Why was the salad naked?

The waitress forgot the dressing.

Why don't tomatoes like to box?

They get beat to a pulp.

What is a tree's favorite drink?

Root beer.

When does hot chocolate cause a stabbing pain in the eye?

When you forget to take out the spoon!

Where does Santa go to buy potatoes?

Idaho-ho-ho!

Why did the kid have string beans stuck up his nose?

He wasn't eating properly.

It was so hot...

...the cornfield popped,

...the cows gave evaporated milk,

...the grapes turned to raisins, and

...the chickens laid hard-boiled eggs!

What do you call a stupid pirate?

The pillage idiot.

Why couldn't the pirate play cards?

He was sitting on the deck!

Why did the pirate walk the plank?

Because he couldn't afford a dog.

Which pirate makes the best clam chowder?

Captain Cook!

Why did the pirate put a chicken on top of his treasure chest?

Because eggs mark the spot.

What did the pirate say when his wooden leg got stuck in a snowbank?

"Shiver me timbers!"

Why wouldn't the pirate fight the octopus?

It was too well-armed.

What type of socks do pirates wear?

Arrrrrgyle.

Why did the pirate buy an eye patch?

He couldn't afford an iPhone.

Why didn't the pirate take a bath before he walked the plank?

He knew he would just wash up on shore later.

What did the pirate say on his 80th birthday?

"Aye, matey!"

Where do pirate ships go when they're sick?

To the dock.

Where can you find a pirate who has lost his wooden legs?

Right where you left him.

What's a pirate's favorite vegetable?

Arrrrrtichoke.

First Mate: Feeding the prisoners to the sharks isn't any fun.

Captain: It is for the sharks!

ARRR!

What happened when the red pirate ship sank in the Black Sea?
The crew was marooned.

Why are pirates called pirates?
Because they just arrrrr!

Why do pirate captains always sing tenor?
They're the only ones who can hit the high Cs.

Where did the pirate leave his keys?
Off the coast of Florida.

What do you call a pirate with two eyes and two legs?
Rookie.

What has eight arms, eight legs, and eight eyes?
Eight pirates.

Where did the one-legged pirate go for breakfast?
IHOP.

What is the pirate's favorite letter in the alphabet?
X...That's where the treasure is.

How much do pirates pay for their earrings?
A buck an ear (buccaneer).

Did you hear about the new *Pirates of the Caribbean* movie?

It was rated Arrr!

Why was it rated Arrr?

Too much booty!

What do you call a pirate droid?

Arrr2-D2

What happened to the pirate who couldn't pee?

He became arrrate (irate).

What's the difference between a jeweler and the captain of a ship?

One sees the watches and the other watches the seas.

How does a pirate know when the sea is friendly?

It waves.

FAIRY FUNNY!

Who helped Fisherella get to the ball?
Her fairy codmother.

Why did Robin Hood steal money from the rich?
Because the poor didn't have any.

Who was the fattest knight at King Arthur's Round Table?
Sir Cumference.

What do you call a princess who falls down on the ice?
Slipping Beauty.

On which side of the house did Jack grow the beanstalk?
The outside.

Why is Tinker Bell always flying around?
Because she lives in Neverland.

Why did Cinderella get kicked off the soccer team?
She kept running away from the ball.

First Dragon: Am I too late for dinner?

Second Dragon: Yes. Everyone's eaten.

Who weighs two tons and went to the ball wearing glass slippers?

Cinderelephant.

Why did Robin Hood's men hate living in Sherwood Forest?

It only had one Little John.

Who carves wooden figures and lives under the sea?

The Whittle Mermaid.

What do you get if you cross Tinker Bell with a werewolf?

A hairy fairy.

What do you get if you cross a hairy fairy with a monster?

A scary hairy fairy.

What laundry detergent does the Little Mermaid use?

Tide.

Optician: Have your eyes ever been checked?

Ogre: No. They've always been red.

FAIRY FUNNY!

Why does Snow White treat all of the dwarves equally?

Because she's the fairest of them all.

How did Jack know how many beans his cow was worth?

He used a cowculator.

Fairyland Best-sellers:

How to Cook Crocodile by Stu Potts

Aladdin's Lamp: The Inside Story by A. Genie

Who Killed Captain Hook? by Howard I. Know

Why can't Goldilocks sleep?

Night-bears!

Why did the Little Mermaid blush?

She saw the ship's bottom!

Why did Rapunzel go to parties?

She liked to let her hair down!

How is Prince Charming like a book?

He has a lot of pages.

What do you call a wee cottage?

A gnome home.

What is Humpty Dumpty's least favorite season?
Fall.

Who stole the soap from the Three Bears' bathroom?
The robber ducky.

What did Peter Pan say when he saw the tornado?
"Look! It's Wendy."

Why didn't the Fairy Godmother laugh at Cinderella's jokes?
They weren't fairy funny.

Where does Robin Hood like to shop?
At Target.

Who's the smartest fairy in Neverland?
Thinker Bell.

What do you call a fairy that won't bathe?
Stinker Bell.

Why is the ocean floor so sandy?
There are never enough mermaids.

Why is the Tooth Fairy so smart?
She's collected a lot of wisdom teeth.

KNOCK-KNOCK!

Knock-knock!
Who's there?
Comma.
Comma who?
**Comma little closer
and I'll tell you!**

Knock-knock!
Who's there?
Interrupting chicken.
Interrupting chick—
**HEY! WANNA
CROSS THE ROAD?**

Knock-knock!
Who's there?
Dishes.
Dishes who?
**Dishes the way
I talk since I lost
my two front teeth!**

Knock-knock!
Who's there?
Ya.
Ya who?
**Sorry.
I prefer Google.**

Knock-knock!
Who's there?
Amos.
Amos who?
A mosquito bit me.

Knock-knock!
Who's there?
Andy.
Andy who?
Andy bit me again!

Knock-knock!
Who's there?
Omelette.
Omelette who?
Omelette smarter
than I look.

Why did the duck
cross the road?
To get to your house.
Knock-knock!
Who's there?
The duck!

Knock-knock!
Who's there?
Stan.
Stan who?
Stan back!
I'm going to kick
the door down.

M-O-O...!
Knock-knock!
Who's there?
Time-traveling cow.

Knock-knock!
Who's there?
Deluxe.
Deluxe who?
Deluxe-smith.
I'm here to
fix de lock.

Knock-knock!
Who's there?
Ida.
Ida who?
Ida called
first but my
cell phone died.

Knock-knock!
Who's there?
Howdy!
Howdy who?
Howdy do that?

Knock-knock!
Who's there?
Euripides.
Euripides who?
Euripides pants you
buy me new ones.

Knock-knock!
Who's there?
Cows go.
Cows go who?
No, silly!
Cows go "MOO"!

Knock-knock!
Who's there?
Interrupting zombie.
Interrupting zom—
"BRAAAINS!"

Knock-knock!
Who's there?
Europe.
Europe who?
What?
No, you're a poo!

Knock-knock!
Who's there?
Althea.
Althea who?
Althea later alligator!

Knock-knock!
Who's there?
Dare.
Dare who?
Dare must be
some mistake!

Knock-knock!
Who's there?
Dozen.
Dozen who?
Dozen anyone care
that I'm stuck
outside in the cold?

Knock-knock!
Who's there?
Topeka.
Topeka who?
Why do you like
Topeka your nose?

Knock-knock!
Who's there?
Pig.
Pig who?
Pig me up after
school, please!

Knock-knock!
Who's there?
Kenya.
Kenya who?
Kenya come out and
play after dinner?

Knock-knock!
Who's there?
Will Hugh.
Will Hugh who?
Will Hugh toss
that ball back over
the fence?

Knock-knock!
Who's there?
Zeeno.
Zeeno who?
Zeeno evil.
Hear no evil.

Knock-knock!
Who's there?
My panther.
My panther who?
My panther
falling down.

Knock-knock!
Who's there?
Ooze.
Ooze who?
Ooze afraid of
the Big Bad Wolf?

Knock-knock!
Who's there?
Weird.
Weird who?
Weird you hide
the chocolate?

Knock-knock!
Who's there?
Yoda.
Yoda who?
Yoda weirdest
person I know.

Knock-knock!
Who's there?
Skip.
Skip who?
Just skip it.
I'll go next door.

Knock-knock!
Who's there?
Tubby.
Tubby who?
Tubby or
not Tubby?
That is the question.

Knock-knock!
Who's there?
Wooden.
Wooden who?
Wooden you like
to know!

Knock-knock!
Who's there?
I am.
I am who?
You mean you
don't know?

Knock-knock!
Who's there?
Saul.
Saul who?
Saul there is,
there ain't no more!

Why do elephants wear tennies?

Because ninies are too small and elevenies are too big!

What is big and gray and blue?

An elephant holding its breath.

Why did the elephant change his socks?

Because they were dirty.

Why do elephants have a trunk?

They would look silly carrying a hatbox.

What did the worm say after he crawled under the elephant's foot?

I'll never have the guts to do that again!

What's worse than an elephant with no shirt on?

A hippo-bottomless.

What time is it when an elephant sits on the fence?

Time to get a new fence.

ELEPHANTS

What time is it when an elephant sits on an electric fence?

Time to get a new elephant!

Why do elephants paint their toenails red, yellow, orange, green, and brown?

So they can hide in a bag of M&Ms.

Why didn't the elephant wear pajamas at camp?

He forgot to pack his trunk.

Why do ducks have webbed feet?

To stamp out forest fires.

Where do elephants with zits go?

To the pachydermatologist.

Why do elephants have flat feet?

To stamp out flaming ducks!

Which elephants live in the Arctic?

The cold ones.

What's big, gray, and lives in Scotland?

The Loch Ness Elephant.

What kind of elephants live at the North Pole?

Elfaphants.

What do you get when you cross an elephant with peanut butter?

An elephant that sticks to the roof of your mouth.

Why are elephants large, gray, and wrinkled?

If they were small, round, and white, they'd be aspirins.

Why can't you take an elephant to school?

It won't fit in your backpack.

How do you tell an elephant from a dozen eggs?

If you don't know, I'll send someone else to the store.

Why do elephants walk sideways through grass?

To trip the field mice.

What's gray and has four legs and a trunk?

A mouse going on vacation.

How do you get down from an elephant?

You don't. You get down from a duck.

ELEPHANTS

What do you call an elephant that doesn't matter?

An irrelephant.

What goes *thump, thump, thump, squish*?

An elephant with one wet sneaker.

What do you get if you drop an elephant on a baby butterfly?

A splatterpillar.

How can you tell when there are three elephants in the bathtub with you?

You count them!

What do you call an elephant that never takes a bath?

A smellyphant.

Why did the elephant paint his toenails different colors?

To hide in the jelly bean jar.

Have you ever found an elephant in a jelly bean jar?

See? It works.

Who started the elephant jokes?

That's what the elephants want to know.

When does a baby elephant look like a cute little bunny?

When she's wearing a cute little bunny suit.

What do you do with old bowling balls?

Give them to elephants to use as marbles.

Why do elephants wear sandals?

So they don't sink in the sand.

Why do ostriches stick their head in the sand?

To look for the elephants who forgot to wear their sandals.

Why do elephants have big ears?

To keep their sunglasses from falling off.

Why do elephants wear sunglasses?

So Tarzan doesn't recognize them.

What did Tarzan say when he saw a herd of elephants running through the jungle?

Nothing. He didn't recognize them with their sunglasses on.

Why do elephants have wrinkled knees?

They tie their tennis shoes too tight.

HUMDINGERS

What did the drummer get on his IQ test?
Saliva.

Who is the wasp's favorite composer?
Bee-thoven.

Did you hear about the cobra that hid in the tuba?
He was a real snake in the brass.

What has lots of keys but can't open doors?
A piano.

Why do bagpipers march when they play?
To get away from the noise.

Why did the rock star bring a pencil on stage?
He wanted to draw a big crowd.

What's the difference between an accordion and an onion?
No one cries when you chop up an accordion.

Did you hear about the band called 1023 Megabytes?
They were on their way to a gig.

What is the squirrel's favorite opera?
The Nutcracker.

What is the rabbit's favorite music?
Hip-hop!

What's Beethoven's favorite fruit?
Ba-na-na-na!!!

Why did the pop star get arrested?
She got in treble!

What song do vampires hate?
"You Are My Sunshine."

What do you call a musical pickle?
A piccolo.

What's big and gray with horns?
An elephant marching band.

Why did the school band have such bad manners?
It didn't know how to conduct itself.

Why are pop stars so cool?

They have millions of fans.

Why did Mozart hate chickens?

They're always running around going
"Bach! Bach! Bach!"

How do you get your dad to drive really fast?

Put your drums in the middle of the road.

Why did the chicken cross the road?

To get away from the oboe recital.

How do you clean a tuba?

With a tuba toothpaste.

Why don't guitarists work?

They only know how to play.

Why did the punk rocker cross the road?

He was stapled to a chicken.

Why was the guitar mad?

It was tired of being picked on.

What kind of paper makes music?

Rapping paper!

Why did the pianist bang the side of his head against the keyboard?

He was playing by ear.

Where do vampire violinists go for vacation?

The Vile Inn.

What's the most musical part of a turkey?

The drumstick.

What was stolen from the music store?

The lute!

How do you make a bandstand?

Take away their chairs!

Why do hummingbirds hum?

They forgot the words.

Why shouldn't kids go to the symphony?

Too much sax and violins.

What kind of band doesn't play music?

A rubber band.

SPACE CASE

When does the moon stop eating?
When it's full.

What tastes better, a comet or an asteroid?
An asteroid, because it's meteor!

Why does E.T. have such big eyes?
He saw his phone bill.

Which astronaut wears the biggest helmet?
The one with the biggest head.

How do you serve aliens dinner?
On flying saucers.

Favorite Space Book: *Full Moon* **by Seymour Buns**

How do astronauts keep warm on the International Space Station?
They turn up the space heater.

How do meteors stay clean?

They shower!

What does an astronaut wear to bed?

Space jammies.

What did the astronomer see at the center of Jupiter?

The letter i.

What's the difference between E.T. and a teenager?

E.T. actually phoned home.

Why did the space restaurant close down?

It lacked atmosphere.

What do you get when you cross a kangaroo with an alien?

A Mars-upial.

Did you hear about the astronaut who broke the law of gravity?

She got a suspended sentence.

Why was the moon acting so loony?

It was going through a phase.

How does the universe hold up its pants?

With an asteroid belt.

What do stars do when they want a snack?

Take a bite out of the Milky Way.

How do you throw the best party in the solar system?

You planet.

What did the astronaut cook for lunch?

An unidentified frying object.

How do you get an astronaut's baby to fall asleep?

You rocket.

What is Han Solo's favorite restaurant?

Jabba the Pizza Hutt.

Captain Kirk: "Our next mission takes us to the Sun."

Scotty: "We canna do it, Captain! The sun is far too hot."

Captain Kirk: "Don't worry, Scotty. We'll land at night."

What kind of songs do astronauts like?

Neptunes!

What do you call a UFO with a leak?
A crying saucer.

What did the alien say to the garden?
Take me to your weeder.

How do Martians count to 13?
On their fingers.

Teacher: Which is closer, China or the moon?
Kid: Duh...the moon. You can't see China from here.

What was the alien's favorite taco filling?
Human beans.

Why did the chicken cross the galaxy?
To boldly go where no chicken had gone before.

Kid 1: I hear Dracula will be starring in the next *Star Wars* movie.
Kid 2: Really? What's it called?
Kid 1: *The Vampire Strikes Back*.

What did the ones say to the twos and threes?
"May the fours be with you!"

What kind of life was found on Pluto?
Fleas.

When can't you visit the moon?
When it's full.

On which planet did the space probe crash?
Splaturn!

What do you get when you cross a toad with the sun?
Star warts.

Where do otters come from?
Otter space.

An astronaut's favorite fish: stardines.

What did E.T.'s mom say when he returned home?
"Where on Earth have you been?"

Why don't Martians drown in hot chocolate?
They sit on the Mars-mallows.

How does the moon cut his hair when the sun gets in the way?
Eclipse it.

ONE-LINERS

Whatever you do, always give 100%. Unless you're donating blood.

A kid goes to the store to buy some toilet paper. The clerk asks him what color he'd like. "White," says the kid. "I'll color it myself!"

My friend told me an onion is the only food that makes you cry, so I threw a coconut at his face.

There's only one good thing about getting hit in the head with a can of Coke. It's a soft drink.

A pessimist's bloodtype is always B-negative.

Whoever invented knock-knock jokes should get a no-bell prize.

A magician was walking down the street and turned into a grocery store.

The time traveler was still hungry after his last bite, so he went back four seconds.

What is the difference between ignorance and apathy? I don't know, and I don't care.

A cowboy, a clown, and a fireman walk into a bar. Ow!

I was addicted to the hokey pokey... but I turned myself around. Isn't that what it's all about?

The wig thief struck again last night. Police are combing the area.

Jokes about German sausages are the wurst.

When fish are in schools, they sometimes take debate.

A dog gave birth to puppies in the park and was cited for littering.

Two silkworms had a race. They ended up in a tie.

My dog can do magic tricks. It's a labracadabrador.

I was struggling to figure out how lightning works, then it struck me.

Parallel lines have so much in common. It's a shame they'll never meet.

THE FUNNIEST JOKES EVER!

If Iron Man and the Silver Surfer teamed up, they would be alloys.

Just went to an emotional wedding...even the cake was in tiers.

Two antennae decided to get married.The ceremony was dull, but the reception was great!

Living on Earth might be expensive, but at least you get a free trip around the sun every year.

I know a lot of jokes about unemployed people, but none of them work.

Why do we cook bacon and bake cookies?

A black hole is a tunnel at the end of the light.

Time flies...when you throw your alarm clock across the room.

A rancher had 196 cows in his field, but when he rounded them up he had 200.

Taller kids always sleep longer.

I was up all night wondering where the sun had gone...then it dawned on me.

I would go rock climbing if I were a little boulder.

I used to have a fear of hurdles, but I got over it.

If a boomerang always comes back to you, why throw it in the first place?

Dad gave me a bat for my birthday, but the first time I tried to play with it, it flew away.

Dry-erase boards are remarkable.

Just wrote a song about a tortilla. Actually, it was more of a wrap.

Always keep a smile on your face. It looks silly anywhere else on your body.

Silence is golden. Duct tape is silver.

Two wrongs don't make a right...but two Wrights did make an airplane!

To the guy who invented zero: Thanks for nothing!

You should learn sign language. It's very handy.

I smeared some ketchup all over my eyes once.
It was a bad idea...in Heinz-sight.

The almond and the pea fell in love and had a baby.
They named her Peanut.

The pet store down the street is having a bird-sitting contest. No perches necessary!

I'm reading this book about how glue is made. I just can't put it down!

Sometimes I'll open a root beer and it fizzes so loudly that it sounds like it's talking to me. You know, soda speak.

I used to have a job collecting leaves.
I was raking it in!

Try saying this three times quickly:
"Take trick-or-treat trucks."

The baby cookies cried and cried and cried.
Apparently, their mother was a wafer so long!

I didn't think I was going to like fencing.
But then I decided to take a stab at it.

ANIMAL ANTICS

What kind of key opens a banana?
A monkey.

What did the pig say on the hottest day of summer?
"I'm bacon!"

Why do seagulls fly over the sea?
Because if they flew over the bay, they'd be bagels.

What do you do with a blue whale?
Cheer it up!

What do you call a pig who knows karate?
Pork chop.

What do cows read in the morning?
Moospapers.

What clucks and points north?
A magnetic chicken.

What do you call a flying skunk?

A smelly-copter.

What do you call a sheep with no legs?

A cloud.

Why were the owl parents worried about their son?

Because he didn't seem to give a hoot about anything.

What's the difference between a cow and a doughnut?

It's a lot harder to dunk a cow in a cup of coffee.

Why did the cow jump over the moon?

The farmer had cold hands.

Why are frogs so happy?

They eat what bugs them.

What's the strongest bird?

The crane.

What has six eyes but can't see?

Three blind mice.

ANIMAL ANTICS

What do you call a sleeping bull?
A bulldozer.

How does a pig get to the hospital?
In a hambulance.

What does a spider bride wear?
A webbing dress.

Why did the canary fail his test?
He was caught tweeting.

Why was the little ant so confused?
Because all of his uncles were ants.

Why did the rhino wear red sneakers?
Because the blue ones were dirty.

Why do seals prefer swimming in salt water?
Because pepper water makes them sneeze.

Where do cows go for first dates?
To the moo-vies.

What's orange, has stripes, and is red all over?
A tiger with a sunburn.

What do you get if you cross a parrot with a shark?

A bird that will talk your ear off.

How is a turtle like a brick?

Neither one can play the trumpet.

How do you make a milk shake?

Give a cow a pogo stick.

Why do turkeys gobble?

They never learned table manners.

Why do skunks like Valentine's Day?

They're very scent-imental.

How do ducklings escape their shells?

They eggs-it.

Why did the chicken cross the road?

The light was green.

Why did the bubble gum cross the road?

Because it was stuck to the chicken's foot.

What looks like a snake, swims, and honks?

An automob-eel.

ANIMAL ANTICS

Why couldn't the leopard escape from the zoo?

He was always spotted.

What do you get if you cross a canary with a 20-foot snake?

A sing-a-long.

Why don't you ever see hippos hiding in trees?

Because they're very good at it.

What did the chicken say when it laid a square egg?

Ouch!

What do you call a bear with no teeth?

A gummy bear.

What's the difference between bird flu and swine flu?

For bird flu, you need tweetment. For swine flu, you need oinkment.

What do you call a man with 50 rabbits under his coat?

Warren.

What do you get when you cross a cow and a duck?

Milk and quackers.

THE FUNNIEST JOKES EVER!

What's a firefly's life motto?
Always look on the bright side.

What do you call a dinosaur wearing high heels?
A My-feet-are-saurus.

Which dinosaur had the biggest vocabulary?
Thesaurus.

What do you call a paranoid dinosaur?
A Do-you-think-he-saurus?

How do you dress for a dinosaur party?
In a suit of armor.

Why don't dinosaurs talk?
Because they're all dead!

What's the biggest moth in the world?
A mammoth.

How can you tell if a dinosaur is a plant-eater or a meat-eater?
Lie down on a plate and see what happens.

Why was T. rex afraid to visit the library?
His books were 60 million years overdue.

What do you call the dumbest fish in school?
Dinner.

Why did the marsupial from Australia get fired from his job?
Because he wasn't koala-fied.

Why did the cowboy buy a dachshund?
Because someone told him to get a long little doggy.

Why did the cow cross the road?
To get to the udder side.

How do you keep geese from speeding?
Goose bumps.

What did the buffalo say to his son when he left for school?
"Bison!"

What kind of monkey likes potato chips?
A chipmunk.

What do you call a sheep covered in chocolate?
A candy baa.

What do you call a girl with a frog on her head?
Lily.

Why shouldn't you play poker in the savanna?
Too many cheetahs.

What's black and white, black and white, and black and white?
A panda rolling down a hill.

What do you call a sheep that dances gracefully?
A baaaaaalerina.

What do you call a cow with four legs?
A cow.

How do pigs communicate with each other?
Swine language.

How do ants keep warm in the winter?
Ant-ifreeze.

What do you call a fly with no wings?
A walk!

Who's a boar's favorite painter?
Pig-casso.

ANIMAL ANTICS

What's big, gray, and wrinkly, and goes around in circles?

A rhinoceros in a revolving door.

What do frogs wear in the summer?

Open toad shoes.

Why do pigs have the best writing instruments?

Because their pens never run out of oink.

Why did the chicken cross the schoolyard?

To get to the other slide!

Do zoos have unicorns in them?

Yes, they're just big and gray and called rhinos.

How can you tell if an ant is male or female?

Ants are always girls. Otherwise they'd be uncles.

Why did the chicken cross the road?

It's poultry in motion.

A horse just moved in next door.

I guess we live in a desirable neigh-borhood.

We hope you enjoyed this special combination of our original four titles!

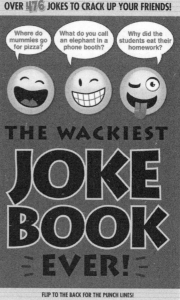

GET CONNECTED

**Find us online to
sign up for our email list,
enter exciting giveaways,
hear about new releases, and more!**

 portablepress.com

 facebook.com/portablepress

 pinterest.com/portablepress

 @PortablePress